A BOOK OF FEASTS

A BOOK OF FEASTS

Recipes and Stories from American Celebrations

KAY GOLDSTEIN AND LIZA NELSON

PHOTOGRAPHY BY AL CLAYTON

LONGSTREET PRESS
Atlanta, Georgia

To our families, who give us cause for celebration,
and to all those who, in the course of our writing this book,
welcomed us into their celebration and their lives.

Published by LONGSTREET PRESS, INC.
A subsidiary of Cox Newspapers,
A division of Cox Enterprises, Inc.
2140 Newmarket Parkway
Suite 118
Marietta, GA 30067

Printed in the United States of America
1st printing 1993
Library of Congress Catalog Card Number: 92-84014
ISBN 1-56352-068-0

Color separations by American Color, Atlanta, GA

Book and jacket design by Jill Dible

An earlier version of "The Family Dinner: A Mother's Gift" appeared in *McCall's* magazine in November 1990.

SHARE YOUR CELEBRATIONS WITH US
If you participate in a meaningful family or community celebration that you would like to share with us, please send your name, address, and phone number and a brief description of the event to:
Feasts
Longstreet Press
2140 Newmarket Parkway, Suite 118
Marietta, Georgia 30067

CONTENTS

ACKNOWLEDGMENTS

For friends who offered early support, encouragement, and professional assistance:

David and Betsy Baker
Rick Brown
Mary Ann Clayton
Lenore and Pat Conroy
Nathalie Dupree
Joel Fleishman
Buck Goldstein
Dee Gurley
Gilda Gussin
John Haber
Trish Hall
Michael Lesy
Sara Nelson
David Perry
Ann Rittenberg
Ron Scharbo
Mary and Wayne Sotile
Mary Rose Taylor
Ruel Tyson
Eric and Laurie Van Loon

For the seemingly endless network of people all over the United States who helped us find and research the stories and recipes of celebration in this book:

Bruce Ashley
Peggy and Allison Engle
Mary Lou and Lou Cutrera
Judy England
Joyce Jue
Yue-Sai-Kan
Ruth Law
Carolyn McGuire
Jane Marimoto
Bob and Lynn Moore
Loretta Nezda
Eric Oleson
Paulette Rittenburg
Blanche and Chet Ross
Larry Wright
Sachie Yoshimura

For the talented professionals whose freely given advice and assistance helped us shape this book:

Atlanta Scholars Kollel
Joan Brandt
Irena Chalmers
Alex Harris
Longstreet staff
Pat Moslow
Alan Schwartz
Jim Wise
Molly Smith

Many thanks, also, to Fuji for their film.

INTRODUCTION

*There is a communion of more than
our bodies when bread is broken
and wine drunk.*

— M. F. K. Fisher

*Live simply, but celebrate special
occasions.*

— Horace

*M*ention childhood celebrations
to almost anyone and the memories
spill forth. The first bite of that special chocolate birthday cake Mother
always spent two days preparing.
The hush that fell over Grandfather's Thanksgiving table when the
turkey was carried in. The well-
worn family stories uncles and aunts
told as they drank their homemade
New Year's wine. The smoke and siz-
zle of the grill as neighbors took
turns flipping hamburgers before the

Fourth of July fireworks. The scent
of cinnamon and almond filling the
kitchen each Christmas morning.
The flowers, the candlelight. Noodle
pudding, hoppin' John, homemade
pickles. The sounds, the smells, and
especially the tastes return as vivid-
ly as ever. ∞ Why are we filled
with longing when we recall these
special memories? What is the
magic of communal feasting that we
find so nurturing? Why are we
intrigued by others who create and
carry on successful celebrations?
∞ These are the questions that
inspired nearly three years of
research and travel as we inter-
viewed, photographed, and feasted
our way across the United States. It
was a journey of discovery. We
quickly learned that nearly everyone loves to swap stories about the
traditions remembered from childhood, especially those that mingle

ceremony and food. And for many,
their enthusiasm in retelling their
stories is not simply a matter of sen-
timental nostalgia. Repeatedly, we
found people expressing and enact-
ing a powerful desire to recreate
those special celebratory moments.
In our travels we discovered new
traditions alongside ancient customs, tried and true recipes as well
as contemporary convenience foods;
most important, we found modern
American men and women whose
commitments to their families,
friends, or ethnic heritage created
times of celebration for themselves,
their children, and their grandchildren. ∞ Ultimately, our journey offered insights into the role
that celebrations might play in our
lives today. In a society of widely
scattered families and neighbor-
hoods composed of strangers, we are
deeply attracted to images of con-

nection. Celebration, the gathering of family or friends to mark a specific event common to the group, can provide that bonding we long for. Even more important, when we meet for a shared purpose, whether a formal wedding or a Sunday night supper, our relationships with one another are strengthened. In this rapidly changing world, such gatherings lay a reassuring foundation for the future, offering a source of support and a network of markers from which we can chart the course of our lives. ∞ Not surprisingly, we have a natural reflex to carry out the ritual sharing of food as part of our gatherings. Since the beginning of civilization, feast days have marked events of the year from planting to harvest. Indeed, seasonal harvests and holidays inspired many of the celebrations we researched for this book. But the role of food in our daily lives has changed from those ancient times. Once the catalyst for celebration, the natural food cycle has been obscured by the ready availability of fruits and vegetables year round in the United States. Most of us no longer eat merely to survive. Eating has

become recreational, food a fashionable commodity. Consumers are disconnected from both its source and preparation. Feast days, once biologically timed to fatten us up for leaner seasons, are now an everyday occurrence for many middle-class Americans. As any dieter can attest, food has become the basis for guilt and obsession. ∞ Horace's advice—"Live simply but celebrate special occasions"—is as appropriate today as it was two thousand years ago. For those of us seeking a better balance with food and closer relationship with others, celebration can be an antidote to our disconnection from both. Setting aside time to celebrate offers us a chance not only to reexamine our daily routine in a new light but also to taste with a fresh appetite. Celebration helps us maintain a moderate diet while we anticipate the pleasures of seasonal indulgences that we share with others. ∞ So how do we create a real celebration, and how is it different from everyday social gatherings? In the chapters that follow, we tell the stories of a widely diverse group of people who shared their personal celebrations with us. What became

evident despite the wide range of styles, methods, and traditions at each gathering was that rituals, the customs that shape the event, and participation are key ingredients for meaningful celebration. ∞ The drama of taking part in ritual is powerful even in the most common celebration—sharing a meal. We anticipate the sweet buttery taste of corn on the Fourth of July, the spicy steam rising from the Thanksgiving pumpkin pie, the smoky tang of summertime barbecued pork. We savor each bite in the company of loved ones and relax into the easy, satisfied comfort of the shared experience. Then we can't wait for the next year's celebration. Indeed, in these moments of sharing, the seeds of family, friendship, and community are planted and nurtured. ∞ The traditional partaking of food also includes less tangible rituals— food for the heart and soul. Some customs are as explicit as a priest blessing an altar of food on St. Joseph's Day in New Orleans; others are as subtle as the jokes and teasing at the kitchen table during the frenzied preparation for that altar. Unlike passive party guests, celebrants do not simply show up to be served. They have roles they look forward to from year to year—decorating, cooking, making sure the routine is followed. Whether best china formal or paper plate casual, whether deeply rooted in tradition or sparked by spontaneity, what guides the rituals and feasts is a sense of shared purpose. The result is a secure framework and commitment that allows some of the normal boundaries between ourselves and others to relax, opening the way for genuine warmth and spontaneous sharing. ∞ But where do we find the time to work rituals and celebrations into our lives? Our competitive society has hurried us so that we feel there just aren't enough hours to keep up. We forego simple pleasures, such as meeting a friend for coffee or walking through the neighborhood, and wonder why our lives lack resonance. Today, even regular family dinners are hard to execute given the complex schedules of active family members. ∞ By contrast, the celebrants who tell their stories in the following chapters set aside whatever time is necessary to create a significant occa-

sion. Putting their busy lives on hold or rearranging schedules, they clear the way for single-minded devotion to the task of celebration. Sometimes the effort is dramatic. Phyllis Bostick, in her seventies, spends almost a year planning the menu for her family's annual dinner; a gathering of friends in Cleveland each Thanksgiving requires many to travel across the country. ∞ In other situations, less strenuous efforts have produced equally meaningful results. The Wampanoag tribe of Martha's Vineyard packed a picnic lunch for their special holiday on the cranberry bogs; guests each prepared a potluck dish for the ceremony to welcome baby Gabriela in Massachusetts. In every case, the point was not the amount of time and effort expended but the sense of purpose, the depth of commitment. Reflecting with us after the events, participants always conveyed their satisfying sense of accomplishment. ∞ In an era when our time is rapidly becoming as valuable as our money, we, too, have an opportunity for a priceless investment. Following the rituals of celebration and breaking bread together allows us to

pause collectively and direct our full attention to witnessing something powerful and real—such as when Phillip Kassel sang a love song to his wife and newborn daughter in a room crowded with their friends and family, when Phyllis Bostick's eyes filled with light as her children toasted her at their annual dinner, when the encircled friends at the home of Aisha Nanji clasped hands and expressed their beliefs about family. In these moments celebrants connected with something larger than themselves and deep within themselves. ∞ We invite you to share those moments in the following stories, photographs, and recipes. We hope you will be inspired to seek your own path of celebration with family and friends, gathering around your table for moments of nurture, joy, and unforgettably good food.

A Note on the Recipes

The recipes contained in *A Book of Feasts* are drawn from the traditions of the groups or families celebrating, and you will get to know the individuals by reading their recipes. Whether handed down for generations in one family or adapted from the rich ethnic backgrounds or geographical region of those celebrating, the recipes offer a taste and aroma of the elements that unite the group in sensual and spiritual communion. Use the recipes as blueprints; feel free to modify them as you build your own celebrations. We hope you'll find that the act of preparing these recipes can be as satisfying as the consumption of the food. If you choose to celebrate with cooking, these recipes and their stories offer a first step to infinite possibilities.

Please note that all temperatures are given in Fahrenheit.

A Book of Feasts

"*It's so nice that the children take part because they're the future.*"

— Helen Manning

CRANBERRY DAY: A Native American Harvest

Gladys Widdis, an elder in the Wampanoag tribe, has gathered cranberries all her life. Earlier this week, she checked the Wampanoag cranberry bogs, fields of low-lying brush on which the small, blood-red berries grow close to the ground. This year's harvest will be light, she warns from experience. "We had a lot of rain in the spring and then we didn't get any more. Cranberries particularly need rain. Usually when you get in the middle of the bog, it's mushy and watery. I've walked all over the bogs lately and the bottom of my soles weren't even damp."

Not that the prediction of a low yield would stop any Wampanoag from showing up at the bogs on Cranberry Day, the major tribal celebration of the year and a symbol of the tribe's revitalized spirit. The second Tuesday of October, the official opening of the picking season, has even become a governmentally recognized local holiday; Wampanoag children are excused from school to harvest and picnic on their tribal land, one of the last wild cranberry bogs left in the United States.

A little before noon, Gladys's son Carl Widdis ("Little Fawn") and his nephew Heath ("Strong Fox") arrive in a pickup truck piled with wood to prepare a fire at the bogs, as Carl does every year.

A bonfire is blazing by the time several truckloads of Wampanoag youngsters pull up. Teenagers and preschoolers, boys and girls, they run down the slope from the road waving their picking baskets, full of enthusiasm for the chore ahead, glad simply to be together again. Some are actual cousins and several attend school together in Gay Head; but many come from small towns farther down the island of Martha's Vineyard where Wampanoag culture has weakened over the generations and where their families live isolated from the tribe

Carl Widdis and his nephew Heath prepare the bonfire site near the bogs.

Teenagers and preschoolers mix easily. Many are cousins and attend school together in Gay Head, but just as many come from small towns down the island where the Wampanoag culture is weaker.

Sassamanesh, Gladys Widdis's Wampanoag name, means wild cranberry, and she has always had a special affinity for Cranberry Day. "When I was a girl, we just took it for granted as a holiday," she says.

in order to earn a living. Today is a kind of family reunion for the kids as they tease and take care of each other.

Though the focus is on the tribal youth, Cranberry Day is not only for children. In the last dozen years, adult involvement has been increasing dramatically. The elders, those in their sixties and seventies who still remember when all Wampanoags were farmers and fishermen, are joined around the fire by men and women in their twenties and thirties. Many have given up a day's pay to be with their children at the midweek celebration. More than a few have not been to the bogs since their own childhood. Now they are reestablishing their tribal connec-

tion, listening in rapt attention as the elders reminisce about the old days, how their parents came to the bogs in ox carts and gathered cranberries by the bushel.

"We picked for two or three days, enough for what we figured we needed through the winter and more," Gladys explains. "The men owned their own fishing boats, and they would take cranberries to New Bedford and exchange them for flour, sugar, molasses. We traded for everything." Gladys pauses, jogged by personal memory to smile. "In my family, after we picked the cranberries, they were poured on the upper level of our homestead, and my grandfather would put in boards so they wouldn't roll out. Those cranberries would stay there all winter and when we children felt bad we'd go up there and run through the cranberries to hear them crack."

As the generations laugh and share memories, it is hard to imagine that the tradition of Cranberry Day all but died out a few decades ago. When fishing and farming began to wane, economic necessity pushed the Wampanoags out of Gay Head. They moved down the island, or onto the mainland where they took jobs in construction, civil service, and trades. Many of those who remained in Gay Head became small merchants dependent on tourism. Tribal customs were followed less and less.

Sitting near the fire, Wenonah

As the generations laugh and share memories, it is hard to imagine that the tradition of Cranberry Day all but died out a few decades ago.

Silva, an elder active in revitalizing Wampanoag customs, explains that although her father was the tribal medicine man, her own first Cranberry Day did not occur until she was already a young mother in the 1950s. With quiet intensity, Wenonah tells how her mother and aunt realized that no one was getting together for Cranberry Day anymore and organized their own little expedition. "My mother said to my aunt, 'We'll go down to the bogs and pick cranberries and preserve the tradition.' For two years there was just my mother, my aunt, my daughter, my two sons, and me." Wenonah smiles broadly at the dozens of children scouring the bogs today. "We took sandwiches for lunch and picked cranberries. We kept the flame. The following year a few more families came, and then it kept picking up. Now Cranberry Day is the size it was when my mother and aunt were young girls. Everybody takes part."

Although picking cranberries is no longer an economic necessity, the "new" Cranberry Day embodies the renaissance of the Wampanoag Tribe of Gay Head, a spiritual, cultural, and political renewal. Most of us do not link politics with spiritual matters, but the significance of the quiet rituals of Cranberry Day to Wampanoags like Wenonah Silva or Gladys Widdis lies in their decades-old political struggle.

For over twenty-five years Wampanoag leaders fought to obtain tribal recognition from the U.S. government and to regain tribal lands. Then in 1987, after being turned down once, the Wampanoags of Gay Head finally were recognized as a tribe. As a result, the federal and Massachusetts state governments agreed to contribute the money necessary for the tribe to purchase 475 acres of previously private lands, while the town of Gay Head agreed to return tribal common lands, including the Gay Head Cliffs, Herring Creek, and the Cranberry Bogs.

In one sense Cranberry Day is a statement of political victory, but as Gladys points out, "With Native Americans you do not separate the spiritual from the rest of your life. You're very involved with who you are, where you came from, and where you're going. We have special holidays or festivals, but every day is a day of thanksgiving."

Though the Wampanoags are understandably private about personal expressions of spirituality, Gladys describes the example her own grandfather set. "We had only the one wood stove downstairs. I remember he'd get up and go downstairs each morning in the middle of the winter. No matter if it was snowing or raining or sleeting, he opened every window in the house at least five minutes. Then he would dance and sing to give thanks for the fire."

Out of such a respect for nature, the Wampanoags have chosen not to weed, fertilize, or otherwise tamper with the two hundred acres of dunes and cranberry bogs they once more control. "During the WPA days under Roosevelt," Gladys

Gladys's sons have all moved back to Gay Head, drawn by their tribal affiliation. The oldest, Donald, is currently president of the tribal council.

Helen Manning began attending Cranberry Day while a teacher in 1956. "I had forgotten, but my son Ricky reminded me that we came down in an ox cart," she says.

TOP: Wenonah Silva comes by her activism and strong tribal identity naturally. Her father, a teacher, was medicine man for the tribe. Her mother lectured women's clubs and YMCAs on how the eastern tribes had been sold short.

RIGHT: Willard Marden has fostered his daughter's connection with Gay Head. "Most Indians, without being able to put it into words," he says, "look at the land differently than most people would. You look at it and you know things, you feel things."

Some work in groups, some in pairs, and some by themselves, straining their eyes to find the tiny cranberries, staining their fingers as they pluck them.

life has always been a juggling of the traditional ways with practical necessity, and this meal is very much a mix of the two. While the kids munch potato chips, the adults pass around bluefish on crackers and small cups of succotash. Maybe it is being outdoors on such a beautiful day, or the appetite that develops wandering over the bogs, or the smokiness of the bonfire, but the simple food tastes remarkably, almost blessedly, good.

☙

Only Gay Head Wampanoags are allowed on the bogs to pick, but everyone is welcome to the evening's harvest potluck at the Gay Head Community Center. As Wampanoag chief Donald Malonson says, "A good way to get people together is to feed them."

The decor is modest. A pumpkin or small bouquet of wildflowers graces each table arranged in a horseshoe pattern along the walls. At the front, a longer table is spread with the autumnal feast. The Wampanoags and their Gay Head neighbors are in high spirits as they look for favorite dishes.

"It always evolves that particular families do particular dishes. When I was a girl we even had men in the tribe who were cooks," Gladys remembers, smiling. "One particular uncle made the best mincemeat and apple dumplings. Then I had an uncle who made molasses cookies, but it depended on the mood he was in when he made them whether you'd be able to eat them or not. He knew everybody loved his cookies, so every once in a while when he made them, he put in more pepper than you ever saw. You'd take one bite and scream. He got a big kick out of it."

Gladys and most of the others who have brought food tonight do not cook by recipe. "We use what is around or what is grown. Cornbread, of course. We do cornbread, not only plain, but in strawberry season we put in strawberries, and in blueberry season we put in blueberries. And because someone in the tribe always had a pig, we always used to have pork and pork scraps to put in the cornbread, and that addition makes a completely different cornbread."

Several versions of cornbread show up this year. There is also a variety of fragrant stews. Gladys brings more succotash. William Vanderhoop, another elder, offers scallops he has gathered himself. His son makes fried

"The drum is a circle, the hoop of life," says drummer Forrest Cuch. "The power of infinity means all things go on. When you're around that drum there is power, there is kindness, there is love, and it goes on and on."

At first only a few young women and girls in fringed shawls sway and nod to the drum beat, but soon everyone is up and moving, weaving a dance of celebration.

dough, which the children dust with sugar. Pat Malonson's signature baked beans are on hand, along with more freshly caught bluefish. There are pies and cakes and a variety of brownies, but no molasses cookies, with or without pepper.

After the eating come drumming and dancing. The room pulses to the steady beat of the tribal drum, which has only recently returned to Gay Head. Like Cranberry Day itself, the drum symbolizes the revitalization of tribal tradition. "The drum represents the heart beat of Indian people," says drummer Forrest Cuch. "When they brought the drum back, it was like returning the spirit of Indian people."

The dancing continues into the night, the spirit unmistakably present. Asking for a moment of silence to thank the Great Spirit for the return of traditions that not long ago had seemed to be slipping away, Chief Malonson speaks for all his tribe. "Although the harvest was small, the remembrance is great."

Pat Malonson, wife of Chief Donald Malonson, is famous for her baked beans, and for the hospitality she shows all who come to the tribe's potluck feast, Wampanoag and non-Wampanoag alike.

CRANBERRY DAY PICNIC ON THE DUNES

Stuffed Quahogs

Baked Bluefish with Lemon

Rachel Malonson's Baked Beans

Succotash

Corn and Molasses Muffins

Cranberry Crumble

STUFFED QUAHOGS

Most *Martha's Vineyard natives who go through the trouble of preparing these shellfish usually have their own special flavorings and proportions, but the ingredients listed below are likely to be included. If you want to sample an original Native American recipe for these delicacies, find your way to the terrace at Aquinnah for a spectacular view from atop the ancient cliffs. This recipe was adapted from* The Martha's Vineyard Cookbook, *by Louise Tate King and Jean Stewart Wexler (Globe Pequot Press).*

8 quahogs *or*
12 large cherrystone clams

STUFFING
1/4 cup chopped red pepper
1/2 cup minced onion
1/2 teaspoon minced garlic
1/4 teaspoon red pepper sauce
 (such as Tabasco)
1/2 teaspoon Worcestershire
 sauce
1 large egg, beaten
1 cup breadcrumbs, dried

With an oyster knife, shuck the quahogs or clams, reserving the liquid. Chop the meats coarsely and mix with the stuffing ingredients, adding juice to moisten. Brush inside of the shell bottoms lightly with cooking oil and distribute the stuffing. Replace the tops on the shells and tie with cotton kitchen string. Bake at 375° in a baking pan, 45 minutes for clams and 1 hour for quahogs. Serve three clams or two quahogs per person as appetizers, cutting the strings to let each guest uncover a clam "package." ***Serves 4.***

BAKED BLUEFISH WITH LEMON

The Wampanoags have long relied on salt pork for seasoning their seafood and fish dishes. It is less expensive than butter and keeps well. In this recipe, similar to those served in many Gay Head homes, salt pork provides flavor and keeps the fish moist in the baking process.

4 fresh bluefish filets for a total
 weight of about 3 pounds
8 lemon slices
4 thin slices of salt pork

STUFFING
4 cups cubed French bread
1/4 cup chopped salt pork
2 teaspoons fresh thyme
2 tablespoons chopped parsley
1 tablespoon melted butter
generous grating of fresh black
 pepper
1/2 cup boiling water

Place two of the bluefish filets skin-side down on a baking pan that is well greased or covered with aluminum foil. In a separate bowl, mix together the stuffing ingredients, carefully adding the boiling water last to moisten all ingredients evenly. Spread stuffing evenly over the two filets on the pan, then cover with remaining filets. Top the fish with the lemon slices and sliced salt pork. Bake in a preheated 375° oven for approximately 25 minutes. The fish are done when the center of the filets flakes easily with a fork but is still moist. ***Serves 4–6.***

Baked Bluefish and Corn and Molasses Muffins

RACHEL MALONSON'S BAKED BEANS

Rachel, also known as "Pat," got this recipe from her mother, Betsy Blain. It is a classic New England recipe that reminds us how much of our early American cooking traditions were based on Native American cuisine.

1 pound kidney or pea beans
1/4 pound salt pork
2 cups sugar
2 teaspoons dried mustard
salt and pepper

Soak the beans in water overnight in a large bowl or cooking pot. Be sure

Succotash

the water covers the beans by several inches. Drain the beans, transfer to a pot, then add fresh water to cover. Cook on top of the stove over medium heat until the beans break open—about 1 hour. Drain the beans again, reserving the cooking liquid. Place the salt pork in the bottom of a nonmetal bean pot or casserole. Cover with a layer of 1/4 of the beans, a sprinkling of salt and pepper, 1/2 teaspoon of the dried mustard, and 1/2 cup of the sugar. Repeat layers until beans and sugar are used up, topping with the sugar, mustard, salt, and pepper. Add reserved liquid to cover. Cover the pot and bake at 325° for 8 hours, keeping the pot covered until the last hour. Check the liquid level periodically and add water as needed.

The final oven cooking of this recipe may be done in a crock pot. After layering the beans and seasonings as above in a crock pot or slow cooker, cover and cook on high for about 7 hours. To finish, place the beans uncovered in an oven casserole for the last hour to thicken and darken the rich brown sauce. *Serves 6–8.*

SUCCOTASH

Succotash, *derived from the Native American word* m'sickquatash *(referring to the whole grains of corn), is typically made with only lima beans and corn. Gladys Widdis, who is famous for her succotash, uses corn, white pea beans*

and salt pork. We wanted to add some of the wonderful smokiness we tasted that day when she cooked hers over the campfire, so we substituted smoked ham hocks for the pork. Succotash is best eaten under sparkling October skies near a Gay Head cranberry bog. Lacking that setting, it makes a wonderful fall supper for family or friends anywhere.

1/2 pound dried navy beans
1/2 pound dried lima beans
1 large onion, chopped
1 (4–5 ounces) smoked or "country" ham hock
2 tablespoons sugar
salt and pepper to taste
6 ears yellow corn or 3 cups corn cut off the cob
1/2–3/4 cup milk (you may use half cream for a richer flavor or all skim milk for a lower-fat version)

Rinse beans in a colander and remove any stones or dirt. Place in a pot or large bowl, cover with cold water, and soak the beans overnight. Drain and rinse the beans in a colander. Place the beans in a Dutch oven on top of the stove or in an electric crock pot with onion, ham hocks, sugar, and a little salt and pepper. Add water to cover and simmer on low heat for about 4 hours, then add the corn. Continue cooking to blend the flavors 1 to 2 hours. Just before serving, add the milk and check seasonings. Remove the ham hock. *Serves 10–12.*

CORN AND MOLASSES MUFFINS

This cornbread recipe uses two ingredients well known to the Wampanoags and early Martha's Vineyard settlers—cornmeal and molasses. The result is a dense golden brown muffin, a perfect accompaniment to succotash. The Wampanoags often add fruit to their cornbread. Try adding a cup of fresh blueberries or cranberries. Another delicious variation is to spread a fruit butter such as apple, strawberry, or blueberry on the warm muffins, making them an ideal breakfast or tea-time treat.

1 cup sifted white all-purpose
  flour
1 teaspoon baking soda
3/4 teaspoon salt
1 1/2 cups yellow cornmeal
2 large eggs
3/4 cup buttermilk
1/4 cup molasses

Resift white flour with baking soda and salt into a mixing bowl. Blend in cornmeal until the mixture is evenly colored. In a separate bowl, beat together the wet ingredients and pour into the flour mixture, stirring with a wooden spoon until just blended. Pour the batter into well-greased muffin tins and bake in a preheated 375° oven for 12 to 15 minutes. The muffins are done when they spring back after you touch the center lightly with your finger.
Makes 1 dozen muffins.

CRANBERRY CRUMBLE

There are many wonderful ways to serve the versatile cranberry, but few methods produce a homier or more satisfying dessert. Gladys Widdis, who, unlike her grandfather, no longer stores her surplus cranberries in the attic, always keeps a supply in the freezer to use year round. We recommend that you stock up in the grocery and do the same.

1/2 cup sugar
1/4 cup flour
1/4 teaspoon cinnamon
1/4 teaspoon powdered ginger
4 cups cranberries, whole,
  fresh, or frozen and thawed

STREUSEL
3/4 cup brown sugar
1/2 cup flour
1/4 teaspoon cinnamon
1/4 teaspoon ginger
1/4 cup oatmeal flakes
6 tablespoons butter, cut in
  pieces
3/4 cup chopped pecans

vanilla ice cream or whipped
  cream as a topping

In a bowl, mix together the sugar, flour, and spices and toss with cranberries. Place fruit in a well-buttered tart pan or 8-inch baking dish and set aside.
To make the streusel, blend together the dry ingredients in a bowl and either cut in butter with a knife or pastry blender or blend in a food processor with a few quick turns of the blade. Add the pecans and mix or process until just blended.
Top the fruit with the streusel and bake in a preheated 350° oven for 35 minutes. Serve warm and top with vanilla ice cream or a dollop of whipped cream.
Serves 6–8.

VARIATION: Substitute your favorite fresh berries such as blueberries, blackberries, or even sliced peaches. You may reduce sugar to 1 tablespoon or less according to sweetness of fruit. Bake as directed.

Cranberry Crumble

The moment just before the meal begins is everyone's favorite. "There's Bill's table arrangement," Iris says, "all those candles on the table all lit up, and we're looking at everybody's faces and it is so beautiful."

THANKSGIVING AMONG FRIENDS

On Thanksgiving eve, downtown Cleveland is cold, drizzly, filmy with industrial grime, and generally not very hospitable—an unlikely destination if you are not obligated to visit parents. But as the group of friends who have dubbed themselves "The Big Five" gathers inside Beth Siegal and Michael Baron's cozily disheveled loft apartment blocks from the deserted central square, Cleveland seems the most welcoming, even the most logical, place in the world to come home to.

"Even when I tell people it's a Thanksgiving tradition, they don't quite understand why I'm going to Cleveland of all places instead of going to be with my family," says Bill Sorrell, who has just driven in from Richmond, Virginia. "'Don't you love your parents?' they'll ask. Of course, it has nothing to do with that." What it has to do with is friendship.

By the time Bill settles himself on a stool in the loft kitchen, Jerry Sealy, who arrived from New Haven, Connecticut, a few hours earlier, is already up to his elbows in bread dough, cursing James Beard (unfairly as it turns out) because his anadama bread is not rising. Susan Puckett, who flew in from Atlanta the night before, has already finished concocting this year's version of her annual corn-bread stuffing. She is now helping

"So many of my fondest memories are of shared meals, preparations, and disasters," says Jerry. "I remember one Easter morning Susan called me in tears. She had left the lamb out over night and it had gone bad. We had frozen chicken wings or something instead."

Beth, the group's designated baker, measure ingredients for a tart. Iris Bailin, whose home across town will be the setting for tomorrow's official feast, is performing card tricks for Beth and Michael's three-year-old daughter, Emily, while Michael, who proclaims himself no cook—"I'm an enjoyer"—runs in and out on errands for the others, including a dash for pizzas to share between chop-and-peel stints.

When Susan drops a loaf of Jerry's

Irish soda bread on the less than pristine kitchen floor, a cheer breaks out. "Our first disaster!" Beth shrieks with glee. "The disasters become part of the fabric of our lives," Susan explains. She is almost buried from view by a pile of bowls and dishes. "Keeping track of them is one of our traditions. It's always very chaotic, and the kitchen always looks like ten thousand tornados went through it." The litany begins.

"Remember that Easter when the lamb went bad?" Iris asks, while everyone crowds around the counter to nibble rescued breadcrumbs.

"What about the Thanksgiving Susan had the flu?" someone else responds.

"How about the year we didn't sit down to eat until 10:30 at night?"

As the stories and good-natured teasing continue, it would be easy to mistake these people for brothers and sisters, for family. But to be part of a natural family you need only be born into it. To remain part of this kind of close-knit group, a family of friendship, you have to commit a certain degree of energy, usually available only during that brief golden period in late youth after parental ties have loosened but before adult responsibilities have tightened their hold.

Bill, Iris, Jerry, and the others are no longer college kids. They are men and women in their thirties

Jerry and Susan will never forget the first Thanksgiving in 1985. "There were four of us," Susan remembers. "Jerry, who'd never cooked a turkey before, went out and bought a twenty-four pounder. We all had terrible colds. There were massive amounts of left-overs. The next year we got more organized."

Jerry has baked eighteen loaves of bread over the last two days.

and forties with grown-up jobs and responsibilities. But they have forged a friendship of rare durability. Their participation in Thanksgiving each year has become both an affirmation and a renewal of their enduring commitment to each other despite obstacles of time and distance. All of which sounds very serious and profound. And certainly these people do have their serious moments, but actually, "We laugh a lot," they all agree. "And we eat."

Fittingly, the web of friendships began in the early 1980s, thanks to that life-affirming basic, food. Jerry and Susan were both working at the *Cleveland Plain Dealer*, Jerry as art director, Susan as food writer. "I had to test recipes for the paper, but I was living in an efficiency with limited cooking facilities," remembers Susan. "Jerry invited me to use his kitchen." Beth photographed the food. Soon she and Michael, the only married couple in the group, became friends with the others. "We represent the traditional family element," she jokes. Bill, who had known Jerry slightly before moving to Cleveland, started hanging around the kitchen, too. Iris, a freelance chef, became part of the mix while helping Susan originate recipes.

Sitting on a step in Beth's kitchen, looking affectionately across the roomful of friends, Iris describes her first introduction. "Susan told me she wasn't sure I'd be accepting of this group. I'm older, with grown children. I think she saw me as being more mature and proper, but every time we got together we had such a good time."

The good time generally centered on food at first. Jerry laughs, remembering how little he knew about food before he met Susan. "When I moved to Cleveland I was still eating the four food groups and Wonder bread," he admits as he checks the loaves of bread he's set aside to rise. "Susan and Iris were always experimenting," Bill says, "and the rest of us were very willing guinea pigs."

A deeper involvement in each others' lives quickly evolved. "We all share a sense of adventure," Susan says. "People with a sense of adventure and a passion for life have a passion for food. We're people who are eager to try new things." Soon they were spending most of their free time with each other. "This group of friends is one of the great supports of my life," Beth says quietly. The others nod. Privately and together, all point to the openness among them, the comfort of being together, and the plain, old-fashioned fun they generate as a group.

"We used to have great theme parties," says Iris, describing a particularly memorable party at which all decor and food were in black and white. "I think it was the planning that was more fun than the parties themselves. We got such a kick out of working with each other."

There have been fewer chances to orchestrate together lately. In 1987 Susan took a job in Florida. Bill moved to Virginia, Jerry to Connecticut. When careers pull individuals to far-away cities, most groups of friends begin to splinter apart. The Big Five have held on by

making a conscious effort. They keep up with each other's daily lives, their romances, job crises, joys, and sorrows, through frequent phone calls, in some cases once a week, always at least once a month. They rent a beach house together each summer. And then, of course, they convene for the Thanksgiving feast.

Thanksgiving in Cleveland has become the Big Five's annual ritual, the one time each year when, like traditional families, they make the substantial effort to be together. Family members who happen to be in town are always welcome. In fact, Michael's parents, who live in Cleveland, come every year.

Strangers, particularly those with nowhere else to go, are gladly received. But the Big Five are the core, the heart, of the festivities. "We call ourselves the Big Five, but there's always about six or seven of us that do the main preparations and then other people come in," Bill says, describing the elasticity of the group. "It's like any big family."

As one of six siblings, Bill has always been partial to big families. "I don't know what I'd do if I didn't have a big family around. The friends I've developed here have become a surrogate family, replacing my real family when I'm not around them." Susan agrees. "We all consid-

"We call ourselves the Big Five, but there's always six or seven of us who do the main preparations and then other people come in," says Bill.

The First Thanksgiving

THANKSGIVING IS PERHAPS THE ONE HOLIDAY NEARLY ALL AMERICANS CELEBRATE REGARDLESS OF THEIR ETHNIC ORIGINS. BUT THE FIRST THANKSGIVING WE ALL LEARNED ABOUT FROM OUR GRADE-SCHOOL HISTORY BOOKS, THE ONE CELEBRATED BY THE PILGRIMS AT PLYMOUTH ROCK, DID NOT HAPPEN EXACTLY THE WAY WE WERE TOLD. THERE WAS NO STATELY, SIT-DOWN TURKEY DINNER, BUT THE THREE DAYS OF EATING AND ATHLETIC COMPETITION WERE ACTUALLY PRETTY CLOSE IN SPIRIT TO OUR ANNUAL LONG-WEEKEND SPLURGE OF OVEREATING AND FOOTBALL. ❧ IN OCTOBER OF 1621, TEN DIFFICULT MONTHS AFTER THE MAYFLOWER SAILED BACK TO ENGLAND, THE FIFTY SURVIVING SETTLERS PROCLAIMED A DAY OF THANKSGIVING—TO CELEBRATE THEIR FIRST HARVEST, THANK GOD FOR THEIR SURVIVAL, AND IMPRESS LOCAL INDIANS WITH THE ADVANCED FIRE POWER OF THEIR MUSKETS. WHEN NINETY TRIBESMEN WHO HAD HELPED THE ENGLISH PLANT THEIR CROPS SHOWED UP WITH FIVE FRESHLY SLAIN DEER, WHAT BEGAN AS A BREAKFAST TURNED INTO A TRUE FEAST. ❧ FOUR ENGLISH WOMEN AND A COUPLE OF TEENAGE GIRLS HAD THE DAUNTING RESPONSIBILITY OF PREPARING THREE DAYS OF MEALS FOR THE 140 CELEBRANTS. NO PROOF EXISTS THAT THEY SERVED TURKEY, BUT THE AREA BOASTED AN ABUNDANCE OF GAME BIRDS, DUCK, PARTRIDGE, AND GEESE, AS WELL AS WILD TURKEY. IN ANY CASE, THERE WAS LOTS OF VENISON, A REAL LUXURY FOR THE PILGRIMS SINCE ONLY THE WEALTHY COULD HUNT DEER IN ENGLAND. THE CATCH OF LOCAL SEAFOOD WAS ALSO SIZABLE, INCLUDING EELS, LOBSTER, MUSSELS, CLAMS, OYSTERS, COD, AND SALMON. AND, OF COURSE, THERE WAS CORN APLENTY, COOKED IN VARIOUS WAYS AND EVEN POPPED. ❧ SOME BASIC STAPLES WERE UNAVAILABLE. BECAUSE NO COWS HAD COME OVER ON THE MAYFLOWER, THE SETTLERS SERVED NO MILK, CHEESE, OR BUTTER. AN ABSENCE OF WHEAT MEANT THERE WOULD BE NO BREAD. THEY HAD NO APPLE CIDER, NO SUGAR, NOT EVEN MOLASSES. INSTEAD OF PUMPKIN PIE, THE SETTLERS ATE BOILED PUMPKIN OR, SINCE THE PILGRIMS' NATIVE FRIENDS WERE WAMPANOAGS, CRANBERRIES, SWEETENED PERHAPS WITH MAPLE SYRUP OR WILD HONEY.

er this our second family. We don't live in the same city as our families, and our Thanksgivings together began because we couldn't go home. Now we make that choice, and my family knows how important this group is to me."

As in any family, traditions have evolved. "We take traditions that we really like and want to keep," Susan says, "and then edit along the way." Most of those traditions naturally center on the preparation of the meal.

Discussion of the menu for one year's meal begins almost as soon as the dishes are cleared from the last. "This is not a potluck," Jerry proclaims. "This is our showcase of the year. We want every dish to be

memorable." While favorite innovations like smoked pumpkin soup and celery root salad have been repeated until they've become standards, there are certain basic dishes that must appear. The turkey always must be accompanied by cornbread stuffing to respect Susan's Mississippi memories. Along with novel variations on cranberry relish and elegant experiments with yams, unadorned mashed potatoes are required. And there are always brussels sprouts. "This is the only group of people I know in which everyone loves brussels sprouts," Jerry says with a laugh.

Iris and Susan, as the most food knowledgeable, do most of the assigning through what they facetiously call the phone planning committee. Although the two usually have recipes in mind, delegated cooks are welcome to attempt their own recipes. "There was a time when everything had to be perfect, but we've mellowed a lot," admits Iris with a wry smile.

"I brought my sister out here one year," Bill remembers as he cuts a branch on parkland near the Chagrin River. "She asked why we had to come all the way out here, and I told her it has to be this spot. It's tradition."

"It's become a joke," Bill says about his meticulous table decorating. "I have a tendency to overdo and they have to tell me to calm down."

⁂

Thursday morning, Bill carries out another important ritual, his annual trek into the woods to gather props for the centerpiece. He has been in charge of decorating the table since the group's original Thanksgiving in 1984.

"When they asked me the first time, I think they thought I was going to take a vase of flowers, throw it on the table, and flop a few candles around it. But being the person that I am, I got a little carried away." He bursts out laughing. "I went to the cemetery and gracefully bor-

rowed," he coughs, "some twigs and evergreen boughs and little branches with berries. Nature's bounty."

He swears he has not been back to that cemetery since. Instead, he's found a bit of public parkland, actually a specific tree, near the Chagrin River. He drives out there every Thanksgiving morning, almost an hour each way in sometimes less than ideal weather.

This morning Bill has corralled Jerry into coming along. Braving gray skies and intermittent cold rain, they tromp through undergrowth and almost fall into a small pool of water in their quest for red berries. The berries prove elusive, but they harvest some nice ivy to take back to Iris's house.

Bill takes Jerry along on his annual trek to find props for the centerpiece.

As more friends gather at dusk, the festive mood in Iris's storybook cottage is enhanced by the scents of burning logs and simmering cider.

Iris lives in what must be the closest thing to a vine-covered cottage in Cleveland, a home you could easily imagine going over the river and through the woods to reach. Inside, chestnuts are roasting in the fireplace. Little Emily sleeps on a settee covered by a patchwork quilt while the grownups unpack the stuffing, the pie, and Jerry's bread, all eighteen loaves. The mood is relaxed, sparked with the scents of burning logs and simmering apple cider.

When Iris puts the turkey in the oven, the final countdown begins. Everyone helps Bill cut flowers and place harvest fruits and candles along the table, teasing him all the while about his lavish ambitions.

And the set table is magnificent, earthy and shimmery at the same time, the floral opulence offset by unmatched plates and paper napkins, used to keep cleaning up easier.

The phone rings, someone asking if there's room to add a friend. The table is packed with place settings, but as Beth explains, "There's always room for one more."

At dusk, more friends arrive bearing their assigned dishes. Mashed potatoes and baked sweet potatoes. Cranberry sauce. Pumpkin mousse pies. And, of course, brussels sprouts.

"Oh no, we forgot the California dip—sour cream and Lipton's onion mix with Ruffles potato chips," Susan, the cooking professional, merrily admits. "It's usually our litmus test of the experience. If hardly anyone touches the dip, we know we've had a success. If the dip is mostly gone, we know we're in trouble." No one seems to miss the dip a bit this year.

While the chestnuts and green bean dip appetizer disappear in the living room, a crucial moment arrives in the kitchen: making sure the turkey is done. Iris takes the bird out of the oven while Beth and Susan hover nearby. "Some years we've been way off," says Beth as they wait for the verdict.

This year's is a near miss. The thermometer registers done, but the juice running out is pink. After intense discussion and study, Iris decides that only a few minutes more cooking time is required. Now comes a frantic hunt for utensils. Jerry has forgotten the plastic lobster plate on which they traditionally carry in the turkey, so Iris substitutes a beloved platter that had been her mother's. The traditions are time honored but flexible.

Shortly before everyone is called to the table, the noise level rises in anticipation. Soon Iris will announce, "Ready," and everyone will crowd the table, eating, sharing spur-of-the-moment toasts, telling stories on one another. There will be the ritual chair hopping, plates laden down with turkey, cranberries, and stuffing carried along from one intimate chat to the next. The idea is to draw out the feast and cram in as much visiting as possible. Everyone will compliment Jerry's bread. Everyone will discuss the moist perfection of the turkey, the incredible richness of the sweet potatoes. Everyone will relish this year's brussels sprouts and celery root salad. Everyone will have seconds and still find room for at least one helping of dessert.

But before the first fork is raised comes the moment that all the Big Fivers agree is their favorite—a moment of silent thanksgiving, individual yet mutual, for survival, for friendship, for all life has to offer.

"It's the pause when we sit down before we actually dig in," Jerry says.

"There's Bill's table arrangement, all those candles on the table lit up, and we're looking at everybody's faces and it is so beautiful, a wonderful high," Iris adds.

"Suddenly," Bill says, completing her thought, "you realize just how good things are."

"When we are sure the turkey is properly done is always cause for great relief," says Beth as Iris checks this year's bird.

While the turkey roasts, Beth shares a quiet moment with daughter Emily.

FOOD TO GIVE THANKS FOR

Green Bean Dip

Iris Bailin's Smoked Pumpkin Soup

Roasted Turkey and Giblet Gravy

Sweet Potatoes with Fruit and Nuts

Celery Root Salad

Susan's Cornbread & Dried Cherry Stuffing

Brussels Sprouts with Curried Sour Cream

Cranberry Conserve

Irish Soda Bread

Chestnut "Pudding"

GREEN BEAN DIP

Planning Thanksgiving hors d'oeuvres for a crowd was easy for the Cleveland gathering—guests were asked to contribute. This unusual dip, adapted from Jane Brody's Good Food Book, *was not only light and healthy but a tasty warm-up to the hearty feast that followed.*

> 1/2 pound green beans
> 1/4 pound onions, chopped
> 1 clove garlic, minced
> 1 tablespoon olive oil
> 1 tablespoon mayonnaise
> 1/4 cup plain yogurt
> juice of 1/2 lemon
> 1/4 cup ground walnuts
>   (optional)
> 1/8 teaspoon cinnamon
> 1/4 teaspoon cumin
> salt and pepper to taste
> wheat crackers or toast

Snap or cut off ends of green beans. Drop in boiling salted water and cook 5 minutes or until tender. Drain and set aside. Meanwhile, sauté onions until translucent in the olive oil, adding the garlic, cinnamon, and cumin during the last minute of cooking. Purée onions in food processor with green beans and remaining ingredients. Chill for several hours before serving with wheat crackers or toast.
Makes 2 1/2 cups.

IRIS BAILIN'S SMOKED PUMPKIN SOUP

Iris adapted this recipe from one she learned from her friend Tim Anderson. She uses apple wood from her own backyard tree to smoke the pumpkin.

> 3 pounds fresh pumpkin
> 4 tablespoons butter
> 2 medium leeks
> 2 medium carrots
> 2 small celery stalks
> 5–6 cups chicken stock
> 1 cup heavy cream or milk
> 2 tablespoons pure maple syrup

GARNISH
> 1 cup apple cider
> 1/2 cup yogurt
> 1/4 cup roasted sunflower seeds

Cut the pumpkin into hand-sized chunks and remove the seeds. Place in a prepared smoker with your choice of wood chips and smoke for 30–45 minutes. Remove and cook until fork tender in covered roasting pan with 1/2 cup of water in a pre-heated 350° oven (about 45 minutes to 1 hour). Meanwhile, sauté vegetables in butter with waxed paper on top until soft. Remove the pumpkin from the oven, peel, and purée the pumpkin and vegetables in a food processor. Return the mixture to a soup pot and simmer together with stock. Add cream or milk and maple syrup just before serving and heat through.

For the garnish, reduce the apple cider to 1/4 cup over high heat. Stir in yogurt. Swirl the mixture into each bowl of soup and sprinkle on sunflower seeds.

For a lighter version to serve at this typically high-fat holiday, substitute a low-fat buttermilk for cream and increase the maple syrup by 1 tablespoon.
Makes 10 cups to serve 10 to 12.

ROASTED TURKEY AND GIBLET GRAVY

Iris Bailin used a free-range fresh turkey for their Thanksgiving dinner, and its meat was moist and flavorful. Because free-range poultry does not always contain as much fat and is never found injected with broth or vegetable oil, a little extra care is needed in the roasting process. Iris wrapped the bird with layers of cheese cloth which she then soaked with melted butter. Frequent basting kept the meat moist while the skin browned beautifully. The method below, adapted from Julia Child's The Way To Cook, *is a reliable roasting method for almost any other turkey found in today's markets.*

ROASTED TURKEY
14-pound turkey
salt
8 cups stuffing
1/2 cup cooking oil or melted
  butter for basting
1 cup roughly chopped carrots
1 cup roughly chopped onions

**Special Equipment: cotton
kitchen string, metal skewers, a
roasting pan with rack, a basting
brush**

Unwrap the turkey and remove the
packages of giblets from neck and
main cavities. Rinse the turkey with
cold water and pat dry. Sprinkle salt
in both cavities. Have the stuffing
prepared and at room temperature.
Stuff just before roasting.

Stuff the neck cavity loosely; draw
the neck skin over it and secure on
the back of the turkey with a skewer.

Now stuff the main cavity with
remaining stuffing. Using the flap of
skin near the tail or a piece of string,
tuck the legs together and tie. To
hold stuffing in, press a piece of well-
buttered waxed paper or foil into the
cavity opening. Using skewers or
more string, secure the thighs and
wings against the sides of the bird to
produce a neat "package." (As Julia
Child says, "There are no rules here:
use any system that works for you.")

To roast the turkey, rub all over
with cooking oil (or melted butter),
and place breast side up in the roasting pan. Roast at 325° for about 4
hours. Be sure to baste the turkey
with pan juices every 30 to 40 minutes. If the turkey seems to be browning too much, cover breast and wings
with loose foil to shield these areas
from too much heat. After about 3
hours, add the vegetables to the bottom of the pan. The bird is done
when a thermometer inserted at the
thickest part of the breast registers
between 165° and 170°. The drum-
sticks should move slightly in their
sockets. Remove the bird to carving

**Sweet Potatoes with Fruit and Nuts
Brussels Sprouts with Curried Sour Cream
Cranberry Conserve**

board and cover loosely with foil for at least 30 minutes before carving.

GIBLET GRAVY

turkey neck, gizzards, heart, and
 liver
1 large onion
1 medium carrot
2 celery stalks
1 bay leaf
pinch of thyme
salt and pepper
1/4–1/3 cup flour

Place turkey neck(s) and gizzards in pot with chopped vegetables and herbs. Add water to cover and simmer for 1 1/2 hours, adding heart and liver for last 15 minutes. Remove gizzard, heart, and liver to chopping board; mince and set aside in small bowl. Strain stock to remove bones and vegetables, taste for salt and pepper, and pour a little over minced giblets. Set aside until turkey is done.

While turkey is resting on carving board, remove excess fat from roasting pan. Mix 1 cup of stock with the flour to form a smooth paste.

Place the roasting pan with its vegetables over medium heat and pour up to one cup of the turkey stock into the pan to de-glaze it. Loosen pan juices and vegetables with a spoon as you add the stock. Whisk in flour mixture to thicken gravy, adding more stock if necessary to achieve desired thickness. Strain the gravy into a smaller sauce pan and stir in reserved chopped giblets. Adjust seasoning and keep warm until serving time.
Serves 12 to 14.

SWEET POTATOES WITH FRUIT AND NUTS

Kelly Clark, a guest at the Cleveland gathering, brought one of the prettiest Thanksgiving casseroles, rich in color and texture.

4 large sweet potatoes
1 cup fresh pineapple chunks
2 apples, peeled, cored, and cut
 into chunks
1/2 cup raisins
1 cup walnuts

GLAZE

1 cup orange juice
1 cup brown sugar
1 tablespoon cornstarch

Place unpeeled, but rinsed sweet potatoes in a large pot, cover with water, and boil until the potatoes are tender but still firm—about 15 minutes. Let cool and peel. Cut each in half lengthwise and then partially slice through lengthwise again and spread open each half. Place in buttered casserole dish. Arrange pineapple, apples, raisins, and walnuts in layers over and between sections. Mix together glaze in small saucepan and heat through. Pour glaze over potato mixture and bake at 350° for 30 minutes. Spoon glaze from bottom of the dish over the top of the mixture and bake another 15 minutes. Serve in casserole.
Serves 12.

CELERY ROOT SALAD

Celery root, while commonly found on European tables, is harder to come by in the United States. If you happen to see the rather ugly roots in your produce market (larger ones resemble elephant feet), give them a try. You may find yourself insisting on their presence at Thanksgiving just like the Big Five in Cleveland.

1 1/2 pounds celery root
1 medium apple
1/4 cup toasted hazelnuts
chopped parsley
lettuce leaves for serving

DRESSING

1/2 cup mayonnaise
1/2 cup sour cream
3 tablespoons dijon mustard
2 tablespoons apple cider vinegar

Wash and peel celery root with a paring knife or vegetable peeler. Grate celery root on the largest holes of a standard vegetable grater or process through the shredding blade of a food processor. Blanch in boiling salted water for half a minute. Drain and refresh under cold running water. Mix together the dressing ingredients and toss with the celery root and apple. Top with toasted chopped hazelnuts and parsley. Serve on lettuce leaves (red oak lettuce is especially pretty).
Serves 8.

SUSAN'S CORNBREAD AND DRIED CHERRY STUFFING

Susan Puckett's stuffing has evolved some distance from her Mississippi roots with the addition of dried cherries and sourdough bread, but she has fun adapting the basic method to whatever is available when she's making it. One thing that's got to be there, though, is the cornbread.

8 ounces bacon
2 cups chopped onions
2 cups chopped celery
3 cloves garlic, minced
2 apples, minced
1 cup dried cherries, or raisins
   soaked in bourbon
1/4 cup minced fresh herbs:
   parsley, sage, rosemary, and
   thyme
12 cups mixed crumbled breads
   (6 cups cornbread, 4 cups sour
   dough, and 2 cups French)
water or chicken or turkey stock
black pepper and salt to taste

Sauté bacon in large frying pan until fat is rendered but the bacon is not quite crisp. Remove with a slotted spoon and drain on paper towels; chop when cool. Remove excess fat from the pan (or substitute cooking oil or margarine for a lighter version), and sauté remaining vegetables until soft. Add apples, cherries, and herbs and toss briefly over medium heat. Mix vegetables, bacon, and breads together in a large bowl and add enough water or chicken or turkey stock to moisten and bind all the ingredients. Season with black pepper and salt to taste. Stuff the inside of the turkey, roasting chicken, duck, or goose and roast according to directions for your chosen fowl; or place in well-buttered casserole dish and bake in a preheated oven, covered, for 40 minutes at 350°, leaving uncovered for the last 10 minutes to brown slightly.
Serves 12–16.

BRUSSELS SPROUTS WITH CURRIED SOUR CREAM

2 pounds brussels sprouts
2 1/2 tablespoons butter
2 teaspoons medium hot curry
  paste
2 teaspoons dijon-style mustard
2/3 cup sour cream
1/2 teaspoon salt

Trim any discolored outside leaves and the stem end of each brussels sprout. To insure even cooking, use a sharp paring knife to score the stem end with an *x* to allow greater heat penetration into the tougher core. (You may skip this step, but you risk having some of the outer leaves overcooked while cooking long enough to get the inside tender.) Drop brussels sprouts in boiling salted water for about 5–7 minutes, testing for doneness with a sharp paring knife inserted in center. (This much of the recipe can be prepared ahead of time. Refresh the cooked sprouts under cold running water, then reheat in microwave.)

To prepare sauce, melt butter in small saucepan. Whisk in curry paste, mustard, and sour cream. Add salt to taste and cook the ingredients over low heat until just heated through. Toss the sauce with warm brussels sprouts and serve immediately. (Low-fat sour cream and margarine work well with this recipe.)
Serves 10–12.

CRANBERRY CONSERVE

The Big Five enjoy experimenting with traditional Thanksgiving favorites such as cranberry sauce. The version below is simple and savory. If you would like to recreate a version similar to another of the cranberry sauces found at their Thanksgiving table, try substituting the juice and rind of two limes for the orange and some toasted pine nuts for the pecans in the following recipe.

1 bag (14 ounces) fresh or frozen
   cranberries (thawed)
juice and grated rind of 1 orange
2/3–1 cup granulated sugar
1/2 cup toasted chopped pecans
1/4 teaspoon allspice or
   cinnamon (optional)

Place the cranberries, juice, grated rind, and sugar in a small saucepan and simmer 3–5 minutes until cranberry skins have popped. The longer you cook the mixture, the smoother its texture will be. Remove from heat and stir in pecans and optional spice. Chill. **Serves 10–12.**

Irish Soda Bread

Irish soda bread was only one of several varieties of bread baked for the Cleveland celebration, but clearly one of the favorites. This recipe is of unknown origin but is similar to a Bernard Clayton recipe. It has a wonderfully smooth texture and slices extremely well.

5 1/2 cups flour (all-purpose or
    bread flour)
1 teaspoon salt
1 tablespoon baking powder
1 teaspoon baking soda
3/4 cup sugar
1/4 teaspoon cardamon or
    allspice
1 tablespoon caraway
4 tablespoons butter
2 eggs
1 3/4 cups buttermilk
1 cup currants
butter for serving

Preheat oven to 375°. Mix together all dry ingredients in a large bowl. Blend in butter with pastry cutter or fork. Beat *one* egg with buttermilk and stir into dry ingredients. The dough will be stiff. Add currants and knead dough for about 3 minutes.
    Divide the dough into two or three equal pieces and shape them into smooth, compact rounds on a

A selection of Jerry's breads

A sense of common roots and history holds Gil Watson's family together.

*W*alking through the front door at Pleasant Hill, Gil Watson's restored antebellum farmhouse an hour north of Atlanta, Georgia, is like walking into a Christmas card come to life. Red bows and greenery decorate every door. Scents of cinnamon, apple, and pine fill every room. Family pictures spill across tables. Hand-embroidered stockings hang from almost every mantel.

The Watsons have two Christmas trees. A small one in the kitchen was cut from the yard and is covered with quilt squares and crocheted snowflakes, much like the handmade ornaments on a tree in a settler's log cabin in 1840. The larger tree in the parlor is festooned with generations of ornaments, handmade and purchased, including one of blown glass from Gil's great-grandmother Emmie's original tree in the 1890s. "When it breaks," Gil promises, "I'll wrap it in cheesecloth and put it back on the tree."

Gil has been decorating since the day after Thanksgiving. He has gathered boughs and berries from the surrounding woods, built a fragrant wreath of apples together with a matching dining table centerpiece, and tied ribbons everywhere. "'It's disgusting,' that's my daughter Emy's comment. She says I have bows on everything. I do, it's true," Gil admits, laughing.

A jovial teddy bear of a man, the

Christmas decorations and family mementoes bring each room of the house to life.

Methodist minister is not afraid to poke fun at himself. But his seriousness is obvious. "My great-grandmother, Emmie Kerce McClellan, was a lovely old lady," he begins to explain, "very determined. As Granny herself said, she was 'the tub that sat on its own bottom.' She took care of herself, knew who she was, and never lost that pioneering spirit of can do."

When she died, Gil was compelled to keep her spirit alive. "I decided I would never let Granny's memory die as long as I had breath in my body. She was also the last of

Gil has been decorating since the day after Thanksgiving. "I love decorating and I love preserving," he says. "I've become almost fanatical."

"My great-grandmother, Emmie Kerce McClellan, was a lovely old lady," says Gil Watson, standing before her portrait with his daughter and her namesake, Emy.

a generation of Kerces, and I recognized that the only way we'd be able to preserve our Kerce family heritage, a heritage of grit and determination worth preserving, was to get together once a year for Christmas because that's what they did back when the nine original brothers and sisters were alive. And since in those days they sang a great deal, I decided we would sing carols, too, carrying on a part of what our family had always done."

Barely two weeks after "Granny's" death, in December 1978, Gil organized his first Kerce family Christmas dinner and carol sing as

an active, living memorial to all she stood for. Every year since, usually on the Saturday before Christmas to avoid interfering with individual holiday observances, Gil has gathered his cousins at Pleasant Hill to eat a meal of family specialties, to tell stories of the old days, and to sing. How they do sing.

Gil has made Pleasant Hill the homeplace for his family. "That was sort of my goal," he acknowledges, "to preserve a place that would be a family get-together place and a way for our children to remember our heritage." In 1985 he bought back part of the original Kerce family land. The following year he moved Pleasant Hill, a house he had found in south Georgia, along with the log cabin kitchen from an antebellum home in Atlanta, onto the property. How he came to buy Pleasant Hill is a budding family legend.

"He was on his way to a revival on the Greenville Road outside La Grange," Gil's wife Carol recalls as she sits beside the parlor tree. "Every night for about four days that fall he'd pass the house on the way to and from the revival. They were going to bulldoze the house and put a gunshop in its place. He couldn't stand that the history of that house would be buried. Every day he had more feelings about the house."

That November, Gil purchased the house for $2,000. It was a great deal except that he had to have the building off the property by Christmas. Such a move would be difficult for anyone but doubly complicated for a minister who had to get through Thanksgiving and

Christmas with his congregation before he could think about the house. With some glee, Gil describes the crisis. "No contractor would even fool with it, and I couldn't move it in sections because of rot. We had to take it down piece by piece, board by board and color code and number every principal board." Carol laughs ruefully, looking around at the ornate period decor that has taken so much painstaking effort. "This was going to be just a little cabin we could relax in on weekends."

Gil began stealing whatever time he could from an already overloaded schedule in Atlanta to work on the house. Meanwhile, Gil's mother, Virginia Watson, who had lived in the city all her life, was ready to retire. "Mother said she intended to go to Florida when she retired and live on plush carpet on the beach. She did not intend to come to Rome, Georgia, and live in

The frying pans that hang in the kitchen have been passed down for generations, like so much at Pleasant Hill.

an old house and a log cabin."

Yet here she is in the log cabin kitchen of her new home, stirring custard for banana pudding in the same pot her mother and grandmother, Gil's Granny, used to stir their custards in before her.

Patiently circling the pot with her spoon, Virginia talks about her own special relationship to her grandmother. "When my mother and father died, Granny came to live with me, and when I married my husband I told him I couldn't give my Granny up because she'd come to be with me when I had no one. Of course, Granny came to love him, and she spoiled him to death."

Granny continued to lived with the Watsons after Gil was born. She was in her late sixties. "I was an only child and spent most of my time with her," Gil remembers. "She'd tell me stories. She was a great storyteller. That's where I got my storytelling ability." Gil, a man of many talents and a lot of energy, occasionally puts aside his ministerial robes to dress up as Joel Chandler Harris and tell the Uncle Remus stories Granny taught him. "And, of course, she told stories about the family." Gil pauses. "I don't know how many were true. She could have made them all up, but they were lovely stories."

The stories centered on the life of a hardworking farm family in the foothills of north Georgia, where most of Gil's cousins still live within a mile of one another and some still farm. Having given up her Florida ambitions and moved back to these hills, Virginia has returned to her

Gil's wife Carol remembers watching Gil fall in love with Pleasant Hill. "Every day he had more feelings about the house."

roots. "I made my first jelly this year, out of muscadines that grow here on the property," she says proudly.

Homemade jelly may have been new to her, but she has always taken her cooking for loved ones seriously, as her preparations for the Christmas gathering show. "I strung about five pounds of beans yesterday," she says pointing to a pot simmering on the stove. She has also made a pound cake and her special version of turkey and rice casserole, and she is about to start her grandson Geoff's favorite, a particularly rich macaroni and cheese, as soon as she finishes the custard. She gives the pot another stir, and the custard is perfect, creamy smooth and ready to pour over sliced bananas.

Less than two hours later, as Gil's son Chip lights a fire in the fireplace and Gil sets out his hot punch, the

"I want them to have real food," says Gil's mother, Virginia Watson. "I know how much it meant to me and how much it meant to Gil when he was growing up. That's why I take the time."

Christmas Carols

If you have ever been lucky enough to join a group of carolers on a chilly evening, to stroll along, candles in hand, from house to house, your own small voice adding to the haunting renditions of "The First Noel" and "Silent Night," later to be invited inside a warmly lit parlor for welcome cups of hot cocoa, perhaps dashed with brandy, you know why happiness has always been the central theme of Christmas carols. They are a joy to sing and to hear. ❧ The term "carol" originally referred to a ring dance, or round, accompanied by a song. Until early in the fourteenth century, carols were secular in nature, their subject matter love, feasting, and spring. Christmas hymns in those days piously focused on the purely theological dimensions of the holiday. However, during the time of St. Francis of Assisi, the lilting energy of carols that told the Christmas story in human terms became a popular expression of joy in humankind's salvation. ❧ Many of the Christmas carols we sing today were composed in England and the rest of Europe between the fourteenth and mid-sixteenth centuries. Although Christmas carols fell out of favor with the educated classes of Britain during the Puritan era, they persisted in more rural areas, and by the early 1800s, interest renewed in what had been considered a dying folk art. ❧ The tradition of caroling has evolved over several hundred years. Originally town watchmen sang carols during the Christmas season as they patrolled the streets, lighting lamps and calling the hours. The watchmen were gradually replaced by professional musicians who strolled from house to house where they were rewarded for their musical efforts. Soon amateurs joined their ranks, compelled by the pure joy and fellowship caroling still offers today.

family troops in, children and teenagers, parents and grandparents. Most are no closer than third cousins, some as distant as fifth. No one cares that the lines of exact blood relationship have long ago blurred. They are all closer in spirit than first cousins in most families.

The cousins set out their dishes, share cups of punch, admire the tree, and talk up a storm. There are the annual exclamations when Ludye Fincher arrives carrying in her pies in special woven baskets. An uncle crafted them out of white oak, measuring the exact dimensions to fit her pie plates for his particular

When all nine of Great-Grandmother Emmie's siblings were still alive, two tables were required to hold all the food for the enormous Thanksgiving and Christmas celebrations. It still takes a table and a half.

favorites, sweet potato custard and coconut cream. "I don't remember when I started making my coconut pies, but it just got to be that wherever I went I had to make a coconut pie," she says, smiling shyly.

The last arrival, Ludye's twin sister, Judye Williams, jokes that it took her the longest because she lives the closest, next door in fact. She places her fresh coconut cake on the side board, and Gil calls everyone into the dining room. Like a strict but far from stern shepherd, Gil orchestrates the celebration without apologies. "It's because I put it together and kept it together that it has stayed together," he acknowledges, nevertheless confident that the tradition has developed its own momentum. "I don't know who's going to carry on after I'm gone, but I think somebody will."

As the family gathers in the dining room, their particular bond of kinship becomes clear. After a short benediction from Gil, the cousins sing the Doxology as they do every year. If red hair or a short temper runs in some families, music is the common thread in this one. The prayer is sung with glorious simplicity, the voices blending in natural harmony. Gil's grace, which he jokes is always longer than anyone wants, concludes simply, "Bless us, our food, our fun, our family, our fellowship."

Now comes the serious business of eating. The Kerces have always enjoyed a big meal. "Granny moved to Atlanta in 1896 or 1897, so we traveled back to Rome for every holiday," Gil says. "In the days when all the original nine brothers and sisters

After Gil offers a benediction, everyone sings the Doxology—gloriously. A gift for music runs in this family.

were living, Thanksgivings and Christmases were enormous celebrations. It would take two tables to hold everything." It still takes a table and a half, and everyone still brings at least one dish. However, Gil points out that one tradition is no longer followed.

"Today the kids eat wherever they fall in line. In the old days the children ate last and the parents ate first," he explains, describing how Granny and he cheated a little on the rule even then. "Being an only child and terribly finicky anyway, I didn't eat but just a little bit of chicken, only the white meat. Of course, that was the first thing to go. So my Granny would take the pulley bone off the plate before it ever went to the adults and then put it back in time for me. All those other children in our family were eating backs, or wings if they were lucky. I always had the best piece." He laughs, pausing with a storyteller's sense of timing. "I'm sure I was real popular."

He still eats no dark meat, but there are plenty of other choices. In fact, the one traditional Southern dish absent is fried chicken. Platters of ham, sweet potatoes, salads, and

The youngest caroler present tonight is Judye Williams's grandson, Will Dowdy, age three.

tea. And no one is shy about seconds.

As soon as dessert is over, Gil calls the family together again, this time into the parlor. They sit in chairs, on couches, on the floor by the tree. Although many of the cousins play piano, Gil does not have one in the house, so Judye's daughter Laura warms up on an electric keyboard. Everyone opens a paperback book of carols, and the singing begins in earnest.

"Oh, come all ye faithful. . . ." This is caroling the way it should be. No one is self-conscious, or even hesitant. Everyone can sing, obviously loves to sing, and they all participate. That is, except three-year-old Will Dowdy, who runs in with the important news that he's just sighted Santa on television. The room comes alive as the carolers' voices rise and flow into a music rich with shared history and the joy they all take in the songs.

The glorious singing is interspersed with Gil's storytelling. "I still put a story in and sometimes two, but I do that in the context of the singing. We'll sing a little bit and then I'll tell a story. Sometimes they're stories I've made up, sometimes not."

This year, after a rousing "Go Tell It on the Mountain," Gil narrates the Kerce family's migration from Europe through Charleston to Barnwell, South Carolina, and then finally in 1852 to the hills of Georgia. "Santa Claus had not yet been invented as we know him," he tells the others. "So Christmas giving was a totally different kind of understanding. I want us to have something this Christmas that is

biscuits crowd the long table, not to mention Virginia's macaroni and cheese, her green beans, and turkey and rice. Gil's cousin Avanelle Brown, the other matriarch of the family, also brings biscuits, as well as succotash and a special casserole made with an unnamed vegetable, a cross between squash and pumpkin, that grows on a vine in her garden. Gil himself has roasted a beef tenderloin, prepared a congealed salad, and baked cinnamon apples. There are deviled eggs, butter peas, and homemade pickles. Grouped together on the sideboard are the pies, puddings, and cakes, including a birthday cake for Ludye and Judye who turn fifty today. The meal is an informal affair. Folks wander from room to room plates piled high. The beverage of choice is iced very much like if we had gotten up on Christmas morning in 1852."

Gil and daughter Emy, Granny's namesake, pass out old-fashioned white cotton stockings, each filled with an orange, a couple of brazil nuts, and two fat peppermint sticks. Other years Gil has given cookbooks, pictures, devotional books, and jars of muscadine jelly. He also always gives each family enough ham for Christmas breakfast, but he does not like to consider his thoughtful gestures gifts. "We don't exchange presents because originally our family didn't, couldn't afford to give presents," he explains. "Let's call them mementos, that's better."

The stockings are a catalyst to sharing as family members talk about their childhood Christmases in more difficult times. John Brown, Avanelle's husband, who grew up one of fourteen children during the depression, describes how his family treasured their Christmas orange, drying its peel over the fireplace to nibble on as long as it lasted. As others tell similar stories of making do, a sense of relatedness, of trust, quietly grows.

The carolers begin to sing again. Seemingly tireless, they sing one carol after another. At first they follow page by page through the book, then skip around looking for particular favorites until the evening closes, as it does every year, with an emotional rendition of Granny's favorite song. Their voices rise, carrying on the generations-old Kerce family legacy:

"Amazing Grace, how sweet the sound. . . ."

TOP: For Emy, the annual Christmas gathering is special because "all the family gets together, relatives we haven't seen in a year," and because it offers continuity. "It keeps going on and going on and going on."

BOTTOM: "I wanted us to have something this Christmas very much as if you'd gotten up Christmas morning in 1852," says Gil, explaining why Emy is handing out white cotton socks filled with oranges, brazil nuts, and peppermint sticks.

A Farmhouse Christmas Menu

Gil Watson's Hot Holiday Punch

Bourbon-glazed Baked Ham

Roasted Beef Tenderloin with Horseradish Sauce

Broccoli and Pimiento Butter

Al Clayton's "Greasy" Green Beans

Spiced Apples

Old-fashioned Macaroni and Cheese

Biscuits

Ludye Fincher's Coconut Cream Pie

Virginia Watson's Banana Pudding

GIL WATSON'S HOT HOLIDAY PUNCH

This beautifully colored punch, filling the Watsons' crystal punch bowl, provided a fragrant and inviting centerpiece for the arriving family members.

1 gallon cranapple juice
1 liter lemon/lime soda (such as Sprite)
1/2 gallon white grape juice
1/4 cup lime juice
2 ounces cinnamon sticks
1/2 tablespoon cloves
2 cups brandy (optional)

Place all the liquid ingredients in a large kettle and place on top of the stove. Wrap the cinnamon sticks and cloves in cheesecloth and place in the pot. Simmer together for 45 minutes over medium heat, then remove the cheesecloth bag of spices. Pour the punch into a serving bowl and ladle into punch cups. (A glass punch bowl is especially pretty, though it will not keep the mixture piping hot. Be sure to place a large metal spoon in the bowl before pouring in the hot liquid to prevent the bowl from cracking.) If desired, 2 cups of brandy may be mixed in at the end to make a flavorful but mildly alcoholic drink.
Serves 15–20.

BOURBON-GLAZED BAKED HAM

Preparing hams for holiday gatherings is really quite simple, and they make a beautiful buffet presentation. Hams are commonly found on the tables of a wide variety of ethnic groups in this country, including Polish, Irish, and traditional Southern families. Most hams available are already fully cooked, and the baking provides a way to add a little extra flavoring as well as a method for reheating. Leftovers and even scraps are great ingredients for salads, pastas, and sandwiches. We used a dry-cured ham from Kentucky to test this recipe; its texture was firm and its taste was sweet and unsalty.

10–12 pound fully cured and cooked ham, bone in
1/2 cup water
1/2 cup bourbon

GLAZE
1/2 cup bourbon
1/4 cup brown sugar
1 teaspoon dry mustard

Place the ham in a roasting pan with 1/2 cup of water. Pour the bourbon over the ham and bake in a preheated 350° oven for 2 hours. Remove the ham from the oven and, with a sharp knife, remove the outer skin. Trim the remaining outer layer of fat to 1/4 to 1/2 inch thickness.

To make the glaze, heat the ingredients in a small saucepan until the sugar is melted and the mixture is smooth. Brush the glaze on the ham and return to the oven. Glaze again after 15 minutes, and remove the ham after another final 15 minutes of baking. Place the ham on a platter or carving board.

Skim excess fat from the roasting pan and de-glaze the pan with a little water or more bourbon and mix the resulting liquid with any remaining glaze. Pour into a sauce boat and serve on the side with the sliced ham.
Serves about 20.

ROASTED BEEF TENDERLOIN

This is another dependable and simple-to-make buffet item. If you wish, you may trim the narrower "tail" end and reserve in the freezer for later use in a stir-fry or casserole. Or if you prefer, leave it untied and untrimmed to provide a few pieces of "well-done" tenderloin for those who prefer it that way. Preheat oven to 400°.

4–5 pound beef tenderloin, trimmed of excess fat and sinew
2 tablespoons melted butter or olive oil
coarse salt and freshly ground pepper

The tenderloin should be at room temperature before roasting. Pat it dry with a paper towel and brush with the melted butter or oil. Rub the meat with salt and pepper. Place the meat in roasting pan and roast 20–30

Beef Tenderloin
Macaroni and Cheese
Green Beans with Horseradish Cream Sauce

minutes. Check internal temperature with microwave thermometer. The temperature should read 115° for rare and 120–25° for medium rare.

Remove from oven and let stand, loosely covered with foil, in a warm place 15 minutes before slicing. Serve hot or at room temperature with horseradish sauce.
Serves 8–10.

HORSERADISH SAUCE

3/4 cup sour cream
6 tablespoons prepared
  horseradish or 2 tablespoons
  freshly grated
1 teaspoon spicy brown mustard
1/4 teaspoon Tabasco
1 teaspoon salt

Blend ingredients well and keep covered in refrigerator until ready to serve.
Makes 1 cup.

BROCCOLI AND PIMIENTO BUTTER

The colors of the broccoli and pimiento make this a particularly festive holiday dish.

3 pounds fresh broccoli
5 tablespoons butter
2 cloves garlic, minced
1 7-ounce jar pimiento, chopped
salt and pepper

Cut off the thick woody lower stems of the broccoli (you may reserve them for soups or purées), and slice remaining flower ends lengthwise in

1/4- to 1/2-inch stems. Drop broccoli into boiling salted water for 3–4 minutes until pieces are easily pierced with a fork but retain a pleasant crunch.

Meanwhile, melt butter in a small saucepan and briefly sauté garlic. Stir in pimiento and heat through. Toss the sauce with hot, well-drained broccoli and salt and pepper to taste. Serve immediately. *Serves 8–10.*

AL CLAYTON'S "GREASY" GREEN BEANS

At any Southern Christmas gathering, you are sure to find at least one version of Southern style green beans cooked, as Al Clayton says, "till there's not a trace of vitamins, minerals, or calories left." Al's are the best we've tasted at anyone's table—and not at all greasy—so we've included his recipe here.

4 1/2–5 pounds fresh green
  beans
2 smoked ham hocks
2/3 cup vinegar (distilled white
  works well)
1 1/2 teaspoons salt
1/2 teaspoon black pepper
1/2 teaspoon red pepper flakes
  (those available from Oriental
  markets are of better quality and
  usually leave out the indigestible
  seeds)
1 teaspoon sugar
1 tablespoon Worcestershire
  sauce

Snap off the ends of the beans and break remaining center piece into two or three pieces. Rinse the beans in cold water and place in a pot with ham hocks. Add enough water to cover half the beans—about 1 quart. Add seasonings, stir, and cover. Bring pot to a boil and then reduce heat to a full steady simmer for at least 1 hour. You may stir occasionally.

When the beans are soft and have lost their bright green color, adjust the seasoning by adding another 1/2 cup vinegar, 1/2 tablespoon salt, and 1/2 tablespoon sugar or to your taste. Let the beans continue simmering uncovered for another half hour or so to reduce and concentrate liquid and flavors. Remove the ham hocks and serve. *Serves 8–10 generously.*

SPICED APPLES

These apples are a terrific accompaniment to the ham or any variety of grilled or roasted pork. For a variation, add 1/3 cup raisins or chopped nuts. This dish also makes a quick and homey dessert when topped with vanilla ice cream or whipped cream.

3 pounds apples, crisp and tart,
  such as Granny Smith
6 tablespoons butter
1 teaspoon cinnamon
1 teaspoon nutmeg
pinch salt
2 tablespoons lemon juice

1 tablespoon Triple Sec (orange
  liqueur)
1 tablespoon sugar (optional)

Peel, core, and slice apples into 1/2-inch sections. Melt the butter in a sauté pan over medium heat. Add the apples, cinnamon, nutmeg, and salt. Cook about 5 minutes, stirring occasionally. Add the lemon juice, Triple Sec, and optional sugar and continue cooking until apples are tender—another 5—8 minutes. Serve hot or at room temperature. *Serves 8.*

OLD-FASHIONED MACARONI AND CHEESE

Virginia Watson makes her own version of this wonderful comfort food whenever her grandson comes for a visit.

8-ounce box macaroni
2 5-ounce cans evaporated milk
2 large eggs
10 ounces sharp cheddar cheese,
  grated (3 cups)
1/4 teaspoon cayenne
1 teaspoon salt
1/2 teaspoon black pepper

Boil the macaroni in salted water for about 5 minutes—until firm but still cooked. Meanwhile, mix together remaining ingredients in medium bowl. Butter a 9 x 13 baking dish or a 2-quart casserole. When the macaroni are done, drain and toss with the milk and eggs mixture. Pour into the prepared baking dish and bake

Biscuits

20 minutes at 350°, or until custard is set. Serve immediately.

Serves 8 as a side dish, 4–6 as a main course.

VARIATIONS: Sauté 1/2 cup coarse bread crumbs in 2 tablespoons of butter and sprinkle, along with a tablespoon of Parmesan or some more grated cheddar, over the top before baking.

For a lighter version, try substituting whole or skim milk or evaporated skim milk for the regular evaporated milk. Use egg substitutes and fat-reduced cheddar. You also may reduce the amount of cheddar to 6 ounces.

BISCUITS

Just like the Kerce family Christmas gathering, almost every Southern table boasts some made-from-scratch biscuits with butter, honey, or gravy to go with them. Here's an easy recipe whose secret lies in the choice of flours. Be sure to use a soft durum wheat flour such as White Lily or Martha White—it really does make a difference. Preheat oven to 450°.

**2 cups self-rising flour
1/4 cup solid shortening
2/3–3/4 cup milk**

Blend the flour and the shortening together either by hand between your fingers or with a pastry blender until the mixture resembles course cornmeal. Gradually pour the milk into the bowl while you stir. Don't add all the milk if the dough seems very liquid and sticky.

Place the dough on a floured board or counter and knead several times by folding the dough, flattening it with your palms, and folding again. Keep your hands well floured if the dough is sticky.

Flatten dough to about 3/8-inch thick and cut with biscuit cutters. Place on ungreased baking sheet in upper third of the oven and bake 6–8 minutes, until the tops just begin to color.

To serve, split each biscuit and butter while hot.

Makes 12 biscuits.

LUDYE FINCHER'S COCONUT CREAM PIE

Ludye has been using this recipe for so long that she is uncertain as to its source, but thinks it may have been adapted from an old farm journal recipe. No matter the source, Ludye is always expected to arrive at family gatherings with one of these pies in her custom-made white willow pie basket.

Bake and cool 1 Fool-proof Pie Crust. Recipe follows.

FILLING

1/2 cup sugar
3 tablespoons flour
1 tablespoon cornstarch
1/4 teaspoon salt
1 1/2 cups milk
3 egg yolks, lightly beaten
1 tablespoon butter or margarine
1 teaspoon vanilla
6-ounce package frozen natural coconut

MERINGUE

3 egg whites
pinch of cream of tartar
3 tablespoons sugar

Combine sugar, flour, cornstarch, and salt in top of double-boiler, mixing with a wooden spoon. Blend in milk gradually. Add the egg yolks and butter. Place the pan over rapidly boiling water.

Cook the custard until thick and smooth, stirring constantly. Scrape down sides frequently. Remove from heat. Add vanilla and coconut, reserving 1/4 cup coconut for topping. Pour hot filling into pie shell.

To make the meringue: Beat egg whites with cream of tartar in a mixing bowl with an electric mixer on high speed. Gradually add sugar as soft peaks begin to form. Beat until stiff but not dry. Spoon over cream filling and top with the reserved coconut. Bake in a preheated 450° oven until meringue peaks begin to brown, 3–5 minutes. Remove the pie from the oven and let cool. Refrigerate until serving time.

Serves 8–10.

FOOL-PROOF PIE CRUST

As the title suggests, Ludye's pie crust recipe produces a dough that is easily handled and versatile. Try filling the baked pie shell with chocolate pudding topped with whipped cream as another winning combination.

3 cups flour
1 teaspoon salt
1 1/4 cups shortening
1 egg
1 tablespoon vinegar (cider or
  distilled)
5 tablespoons water

Place the dry ingredients in a mixing bowl and blend in shortening with pastry blender or cut in with knives until mixture resembles coarse cornmeal. Blend together remaining ingredients and mix rapidly with a fork into flour and shortening mixture. Place the dough on a floured surface and knead a few times to finish blending. Divide into two equal pieces, wrap in plastic, and refrigerate at least 1 hour or up to 2 weeks.

When ready to bake the crust, place the dough on a lightly floured surface and roll out into an 11-inch circle. Place the circle of dough into a 9-inch pie tin and trim the edges. Pinch the dough together between fingers to decorate edge. Pierce the bottom of the dough with a fork to allow steam to escape when baking.

Place the pie shell in a preheated 375° oven for about 12 minutes, or until edges are evenly browned and bottom is lightly colored. Let the shell cool on a rack before filling.
Makes two 9-inch crusts.

VIRGINIA WATSON'S BANANA PUDDING

This luscious dessert is truly an old-fashioned comfort food. Virginia Watson does not cut any corners to reduce calories or cholesterol, and we don't recommend that you make any substitutions either—this is how banana pudding was meant to be.

3 large or 4 medium bananas,
  ripe but firm
1/2 12-ounce box vanilla wafers
2 1/2 cups milk
5 ounces evaporated milk
1/2 cup sugar
pinch salt
2 large eggs, separated
1 egg white
1/2 cup self-rising flour
1 teaspoon vanilla
2 tablespoons sugar

With a paring knife, peel and gently scrape bananas to remove starchy strings. Slice bananas into 1/4 slices and layer with vanilla wafers in a pyrex or oven-proof ceramic bowl, and repeat until used up. Be sure to save a few to line the top edges as a pretty border garnish.

Heat the milk, evaporated milk, 1/2 cup sugar, salt, and beaten egg yolks together in a heavy-bottomed saucepan over medium heat. Mix the flour and enough water together to make a paste (about 1/4 cup water) and whisk mixture into the warming custard sauce. Stir constantly with whisk or wooden spoon until mixture thickens to coat a

spoon, taking care not to let it boil or scorch, as the eggs will scramble. Add vanilla and pour over the bananas and vanilla wafers, gently pushing bananas and wafers to allow custard to penetrate and spread throughout the bowl. Set aside.

Whip the 3 egg whites with 2 tablespoons of sugar with an electric mixture on high speed until soft peaks form. Spoon mixture over top of pudding, using a spatula to make decorative peaks. Bake in a preheated 450° oven for 3–5 minutes until meringue peaks begin to color. Either serve immediately warm or refrigerate until serving time.
Serves 8–10.

Pound Cake and Banana Pudding

The Nanjis prepare their altar.

KWANZA:* A New Tradition Honoring African Roots

It is nightfall on December 29. The fourth day of Kwanza. Ujaama. The day of Family. Six-year-old Soumayah Nanji and her five-year-old sister, Almaz, their feet kicking rhythmically back and forth, sit close together on their living room couch beneath a map of Africa. Dressed in brightly colored robes and headdresses, surrounded by an impressive collection of art objects from Africa, the Caribbean, and Latin America, the bright-eyed, giggly little girls are barely able to wait for tonight's feast to begin. The children's patience is impressive considering they have fasted since daybreak, a Nanji family tradition during Kwanza, and since the Nanjis have delayed their feast plans twice already due to scheduling conflicts and family illness.

"We almost said, forget it, period," their mother Aisha admits while she checks the girls' elaborate headwraps. "But my kids wouldn't let us. They'd been going around the house for two weeks singing the song, 'Kwanza is a holiday,' and they said, 'We're not going to have Kwanza? We've got to have Kwanza.'"

As she hugs her daughters, Aisha's excitement matches theirs. A linguist and college teacher, Aisha has always taken celebration, particularly African-

American celebration, very seriously. She has even published a book on the subject. Kwanza has been an important part of her spiritual life since she and her mother organized their first celebration in the late sixties when Aisha was still a young girl.

Over the years, celebrating with her husband, Taji, and an extended family of relatives and friends, Aisha has watched the holiday evolve. Kwanza began in 1966, when Professor Maulano Karenga sought to celebrate African-Americans' cultural heritage by synthesizing customs and values of the African harvest. "When Kwanza first began," Aisha explains, "it had political overtones. It was back in the sixties and Karenga was part of the movement for the liberation of African people." Now the Nanjis interpret the rituals Dr. Karenga suggested with respect but also with flexibility. They decorate. They pay homage. They certainly feast. They bring to their Kwanza a sense of purpose and an intense, infectious joy. "It is still politically conscious, but it is also festive. You can really enjoy yourself now."

Recorded music from Kenya

Soumayah proudly does her own head wrap, called a khanga. Although hers is a simplified version, there is a secret way to wrap.

*The name of this holiday has several different English spellings. Aisha Nanji, who is a linguist, uses *Kwanza*.

Kwanza's Beginnings and Evolution

When we think about successful holiday traditions, we assume an extended history of food, customs, and routines handed down and amplified from one generation to the next. Kwanza, born only twenty-five years ago with all its symbols and rituals in place, makes us rethink that assumption. ⤸ In 1966, Maulano Karenga, a professor of black studies at the University of California, created a holiday he called Kwanza ("first fruits" in Kiswahili) to emphasize the African-American cultural heritage. Synthesizing customs and values of the harvest celebrations found throughout Africa, Dr. Karenga mapped out a complete celebration in which every element represents a specific principle. On each of the seven nights, from December 26 until January 1, a lit candle represents the principle of that day. ⤸ December 26 Umoja, unity or oneness ⤸ December 27 Unjiagulia, self-determination ⤸ December 28 Ujima, work done with the assistance of neighbors ⤸ December 29 Ujaama, family, society, a gathering ⤸ December 30 Nia, purpose ⤸ December 31 Uumba, creativity ⤸ January 1 Imani, faith ⤸ The altar must include the following symbols:

◆ A Kinara—a candleholder to hold seven candles

◆ A Mkeka—a mat of braided straw

◆ Mishumaa—candles, which are usually red, green, and black, but the Nanjis and others often add yellow as well

◆ Mazeo—crops, represented by fruit and nuts

◆ Muhini—ears of corn, representing the children

◆ Kikombe—the unity cup

◆ Zawadi—gifts

Increasingly across the United States, African-Americans are developing their own Kwanza traditions within the structure formulated by Dr. Karenga. The process is not so different, really, from what all of us experience as we find our own way to establish or reestablish traditions, whatever our cultural or ethnic roots.

somebody else has no job. Everybody comes, and it's a time of fellowship."

Aromas sweet and savory begin to fill the Nanji's modest bungalow. The dishes include recipes that originated in Africa as well as foods that have been part of the black experience in the Caribbean, Latin America, and the United States. A dish of chicken and potatoes with curry is accompanied by a pilaf of basmati rice with golden raisins and currants. There are salads and fruit and gingerbread for dessert. Each arriving guest places the food he or she has brought on a table by the front door. While pork and alcoholic beverages are not served in the Nanji household, there are no other rules. Aisha asks only that people bring what they can to share.

Presiding over the bountiful, communal meal central to Kwanza

The Nanjis, who practice no formal religion, do not celebrate Christmas. "We're definitely not trying to do Christmas through Kwanza, but we are trying to make sure the fun things are there," said Aisha, who admits she loves to give her daughters dolls as well as educational presents during Kwanza.

"One of the most important aspects of Kwanza is sharing," says Aisha. She has prepared a small gift basket for each family at her Kwanza feast.

comes naturally to Aisha. "When I was growing up we always had fifteen people at our dinner table, although there were only a few of us in our immediate family. Some my mom pulled, some we grabbed from someplace. And the interesting thing is that the people were never all black. They were always white and black. That is just my mom. She knew who she was so she could appreciate other people. And she loved to cook. So we would have as much food as we could eat and that's an important part of Kwanza festivity: to prepare your favorite dishes and share them."

But before the feast comes the ceremony. The first order of business is gift giving. The schedule for opening presents varies for the Nanjis. Some years they wait to open them all until December 31, the day of creativity, or January 1, Imani, the day of Faith. This year Aisha has given her children one gift every day. As the house becomes crowded with celebrants, the children's excitement overflows and Aisha softens the rules, allowing them to open all their gifts. As much as possible the Nanjis choose presents that have educational value or African-American cultural significance—a pencil box decorated with an African map, for instance, or a Kwanza coloring book—but Aisha also wants her daughters to receive dolls. The

After the arrival of Taji's brother Reuben, Soumayah leads everyone in exuberant singing, acting out the words with her hands as she sings.

children shriek with joy as they unwrap box after box.

Aisha has also prepared a small gift for each of the families present. A long woven basket she bought in Jamaica holds smaller baskets, and inside each is a packet of herbal tea. "One of the most important aspects of Kwanza is sharing," Aisha explains. "If I give you a gift, it means that I'm thinking of you, and if you offer me a gift, I'll accept it because I know you are sharing with me."

Once all the gifts have been exchanged, everyone gathers around the altar to begin the formal ceremony, one of Aisha's two favorite moments during Kwanza. "The first is not really a moment," she says, "but extends over a long period of time. That's when my children start singing the song and asking me to set up the kinara, the altar. That is exciting, to play with the fruit and put up the candles. The second moment, though, is when we do the circle. We light the candles. Everybody's so quiet and we just thank God for allowing us to exist and to coexist. Then we talk about the principle of the day. People are thoughtful. They really think before they speak. Even the children have an opportunity to share."

Soumayah is lifted up to light the first candle in the name of Unity. Then she and Leila Hodge, the eldest present, together light the second candle to represent self-determination. A visiting teenager lights the third, the candle for collective work and responsibility.

Finally, after a bit of hesitation, Almaz shyly takes her turn, lighting the fourth candle in the name of Ujaama, which Aisha translates for her as family.

Quietly, almost formally, the Nanjis and their friends form a circle. While Hassan Ortiz, a professional percussionist, plays his tumbarodora, or conga drums, softly in the background, Aisha fills the unity cup with juice and begins to discuss the meaning of Kwanza.

Suddenly everyone is startled to hear a knock on the front door. Taji's brother Reuben Hawkins and his wife Burnette burst in loaded down with presents. Although Reuben had mentioned to Taji that he would try to stop by on their way home to Alabama from a visit with Taji and Reuben's parents in New Jersey, no definite itinerary had been set. Their arrival on this night and at this particular moment is serendipitous, almost magical.

A rush of adrenalin fills the room. The group sings a couple of exuberant Kwanza songs led by Soumayah, who acts out the words with her hands as she sings. Then everyone gathers again in the circle and takes each other's hands. Someone offers a short prayer. Then Aisha raises the unity cup once more and, with Reuben and Burnette's arrival on everyone's mind, asks that each member of the group take a sip from the cup, before sharing what family, ujaama, means to him or her. As the cup slowly makes its way around the room, the speakers build a verbal

mosaic, punctuated by drumbeats, of what family is and can do:

"Family means the foundation of our family, our community, our nation, our race."

"Once families can get along with each other, then communities, cities, nations can learn to get along."

"Family is the institution that makes it possible for us to keep on keeping on."

"Family is knowing we can agree to disagree."

Even Soumayah has something to add to encouraging applause. "It means to me I love my whole family."

The cup comes back full circle to Aisha, the last to speak.

"My child is your child and your child is my child. And even when we get to be adults, we are still children in many ways and we must look to the elders for their wisdom. Family, the extended family, is the African way of life. You can't run from it, you can't hide from it. You have it in your soul. This is family. I love you all."

Hassam pounds the drum, everyone laughs and claps and embraces. "Now," Aisha raises her voice above the happy commotion. "Let's feast."

FLAVORS OF AFRICA

African-American culinary traditions are drawn from many cultures and food sources. Caribbean fruits and fish blend with east African curries, South American and Hispanic flavorings, and indigenous American crops. While our Kwanza menu reflects only a minuscule portion of this heritage, you may also find its influences in recipes from the Trice Family Reunion and the Watson Christmas gathering (Fried Chicken, Green Beans, and Coconut Cream Pie) because African-American cooking forms much of the basis for Southern regional cooking.

AISHA'S KWANZA DELIGHT

A spontaneous cook who seldom uses recipes, Aisha Nanji serves variations of this recipe as a main course salad. We recommend trying this adaptation as an appetizer spread on whole wheat crackers.

2 6-ounce cans water-packed
   white tuna
1/4 teaspoon cumin
1/2 teaspoon medium curry
   powder
1/2 teaspoon garlic salt
1/2 cup finely chopped onion
1/2 cup mayonnaise
salt and black pepper
1/4 cup raisins
1/2 cup green seedless grapes,
   cut in half
1/4 cup chopped toasted almonds

Drain the water from the tuna

and flake the tuna into a mixing bowl. Stir in seasonings, onions, and mayonnaise. Season with salt and pepper to taste. Fold in raisins, grapes and almonds. Refrigerate several hours before serving.
Serves 4–6.

SPICY PEANUT SOUP

This is a quick and simple version of a classic Southern recipe whose roots are clearly African-American. The peanut butter acts as a creamy, natural thickener, so there is no need for other starches or dairy products.

2 1/2 tablespoons peanut oil
3/4 cup diced onions
3/4 cup diced carrots
3/4 cup diced celery
1/2 cup diced red bell pepper
2 cloves garlic, minced
4 1/2 cups chicken stock
   (canned or homemade)
1/2 teaspoon cayenne pepper
1 cup peanut butter, natural
   crunchy style (no sugar or other
   additives)

Heat peanut oil in a heavy bottomed saucepan or pot and sauté onions, carrots, bell pepper, and celery over moderate heat until soft and translucent. Stir in garlic and toss for a minute or two with the vegetables without browning.

Add the stock, peanut butter, and cayenne. Bring the soup to a boil, then reduce heat and simmer, stir-

ring frequently for 15 to 20 minutes. Ladle the soup into warm soup bowls.
Serves 8.

AFRICAN CHICKEN STEW

Aisha serves this communally on a large platter with rice in the middle, the stew on the sides, and banana or plantain as garnishes.

1/2 cup cooking oil (olive or
   peanut)
1 tablespoon curry powder
1 cup all-purpose flour
1/2 teaspoon salt
1/4 teaspoon pepper
3 pounds chicken pieces
   (legs, thighs, wings, breasts)
1 cup chopped onion
2 tablespoons curry powder or
   medium hot curry paste
3 ounces tomato paste (1/2 small
   can)
2 tablespoons sugar
28 ounces whole tomatoes,
   canned, with their juice
2 cups chicken stock or water
juice of 1/2 lemon
grated rind of one lemon
1 pound diced and peeled
   potatoes
1 cup fresh or frozen peas

Heat the oil in a large skillet or dutch oven until hot but not smoking. Mix the flour with the curry powder, salt, and pepper. Place the flour mixture in a paper bag and shake the chicken pieces in it a few

Baked Curried Perch Filets
Basmati Rice with Currants and Raisins

at a time, or place flour mixture in large shallow plate and dredge chicken pieces, shaking off excess flour. Sauté chicken pieces in skillet until brown on each side. Set aside on a plate covered with paper towels until all the batches are done.

(NOTE: Before cooking, you may divide breast and thighs in half again with a large cleaver or chef's knife. This makes buffet serving easier and increases the number of servings for a crowd.)

Remove any excess fat from the skillet and sauté onions briefly in the pan. Stir in the curry paste or powder. Then add all remaining ingredients, except potatoes and peas. Stir together and return the chicken to the pot. Simmer the stew on top of the stove for 1 hour on medium-low heat. Add potatoes and simmer another 30 minutes. Add the peas; simmer an additional 15 minutes before serving. Check for seasoning. Serve with Basmati Rice with Currants and Raisins.
Serves 8.

BASMATI RICE WITH CURRANTS & RAISINS

Basmati rice, with its fragrance and delicate texture, is a perfect vehicle for the sweet and savory flavorings of this dish. If it is not available in your local grocery, it's worth a trip to an Indian or Middle Eastern market to find it.

> 2 tablespoons olive oil
> 1 teaspoon garlic, minced

> 2 1/2 teaspoons cumin
> 1 teaspoon coriander
> 4 cups chicken stock or water
> 2 cups basmati rice
> 3/4 cup golden raisins and/or currants
> salt and freshly ground black pepper to taste

In a saucepan, briefly sauté garlic in oil, then stir in cumin and coriander. Add the chicken stock or water and bring to a boil. Add the rice. Stir, then simmer until liquid is absorbed—about 8 minutes. Stir in raisins and currants, check for seasonings, and let stand a few minutes before serving.
Serves 6–8.

BAKED CURRIED PERCH FILETS

This dish makes a colorful and easy-to-serve addition to a Kwanza buffet. A variation would be to bake the filets over a layer of sautéed greens, such as mustard kale or spinach.

> 1 cup plain yogurt, regular or low fat
> 3 tablespoons lemon juice
> 2 teaspoons grated fresh ginger
> 3 cloves garlic, minced
> 1 teaspoon cumin
> 1 teaspoon turmeric
> 1/2 teaspoon cayenne pepper
> 1/2 teaspoon ground fennel
> 1 1/2 pounds fresh perch filets, about eight pieces

Mix together yogurt and seasonings in a small bowl to make a marinade, and brush on perch filets. Place filets in a shallow dish; cover and refrigerate for 3–4 hours. Butter a shallow baking pan and place filets in pan in a single layer. Bake in a preheated 350° oven for 8–10 minutes. Serve immediately with Basmati Rice with Currants and Raisins, lemon slices, and your favorite fruit chutney (mango is especially good) or hot relish, like chow chow.
Serves 6.

STEWED OKRA AND TOMATOES

Okra is indigenous to Africa. A wonderful summertime variation of this recipe is to use fresh, vine-ripe, seeded, and chopped tomatoes, which aren't available at Kwanza time.

> 1 pound okra
> 1 tablespoon cooking oil
> 1 cup onion, chopped
> 1/2 teaspoon cinnamon
> 28 ounces canned whole tomatoes, coarsely chopped
> salt and pepper to taste

Slice off both ends of the okra and cut pods into 1/2-inch pieces. In a medium saucepan, heat oil and sauté onions until soft and translucent over medium heat. Add cinnamon, tomatoes, and okra and simmer over low heat for 30 minutes. Add salt and pepper to taste and serve.
Serves 10.

"First Fruits" Salad

This fruit salad offers both a tasty symbol for the holiday and is in keeping with the healthy and natural foods that Aisha likes to feed her family. The fruits listed below are generally available at Kwanza time and are a well-flavored combination, but choose whatever fruits look good at your market and can be depended on to be ripe and flavorful. Seedless grapes, raisins, mangos, pomegranates, dates, and coconut flakes all make good substitutions or additions to the basic recipe. For a sweeter marinade, add more honey or decrease the lime juice.

A mixture of fresh fruits, such as:
3 kiwi, sliced
1/2 pound cherries, stemmed and pitted
2 seedless oranges, peeled, sliced, and quartered
1 pineapple, peeled, cored, and cut into chunks
1 star fruit, sliced

MARINADE
1/4 cup lime juice
1–1 1/2 teaspoons fresh ginger, peeled and minced
1/4 cup honey

Place prepared fruits in a large bowl. In a separate bowl, mix the marinade ingredients and pour over fruit. Toss together and serve in a large bowl, in carved melon baskets, or in pineapple boats. *Serves 8–10.*

Gingerbread

Here's an example of how holiday traditions of different cultures can overlap. Gingerbread is just as likely to be found at a Christmas gathering as on a Kwanza table.

2 1/3 cups all-purpose flour
1/2 teaspoon salt
1 1/2 teaspoons baking soda
1 teaspoon ground ginger
1 teaspoon cinnamon
1/4 teaspoon cloves
1/4 teaspoon nutmeg
1/3 cup plus 1 tablespoon (3 ounces) cooking oil or margarine
1 cup molasses (do not use blackstrap)
2/3 cup buttermilk

Sift together the dry ingredients into a large mixing bowl. Place margarine or cooking oil in a saucepan with the molasses and bring to a boil. Carefully stir in the buttermilk, blending the ingredients. Add the saucepan liquids to the dry ingredients and beat together thoroughly. Pour the batter into a greased 9-inch square cake pan. Bake in a preheated oven at 350° for about 50 minutes. The cake is done when a toothpick inserted into the middle comes out clean. Serve the cake cut in squares. It can accompany the fruit salad above or be served alone—either warm or cold, with a dollop of whipped cream if desired. *Serves 12.*

"*Gabriela is someone
I would do anything for,*"
says Philip Kassel simply.

WELCOME, GABRIELA! An International Celebration of Birth

Most of the celebrations in this book are traditional rituals that have evolved over years of observance. But impromptu celebrations that arise at major milestones in our lives can be the most meaningful of all. And what milestone is more important or powerful than the birth of a child? Two weeks after the birth of their daughter, Philip Kassel and his wife, Iris Gomez, gather family and friends to welcome into the world Gabriela Catherine Kassel Gomez.

Under a cold, leaden sky, slush borders the sidewalk leading to the old house in Concord, Massachusetts, where Philip and Iris have a duplex apartment. Despite a few colored balloons bobbing gamely in the wind above the porch, the mood is midwinter somber. But beyond the heavy oak door, the atmosphere turns lively and warm.

Philip's voice is still strong with a sense of wonder over the birth of Gabriela. "People told me to expect overpowering instincts, but I wondered. Then came the birth. Suddenly I had a totally helpless young person in my hands, and I knew she was someone I would do anything for."

Iris, equally enraptured, laughs. "I'm sure everyone thinks their kid is cute, but Gabriela is *really* cute." She admits one motive for inviting so many of her friends to meet

Gabriela this evening is less than spiritual: "I want to show her off." She also wants to involve her community of friends in Gabriela's life through an evening of ritual sharing. Instead of baby gifts, visitors tonight will offer food from their heritage, lullabies from their childhoods, and written wishes for Gabriela's future.

If Iris seems remarkably relaxed for a new mother about to have sixty people drop by, it's because she and Philip have had to handle very few of the preparations. "I don't feel any anxiety. I'm just grate-

Philip Kassel was swept away by overpowering instincts to care for his new daughter, he says, standing with his mother-in-law, Irys Gomez, with little Gabriela in his arms. "You have awesome emotions for someone you just met."

Outside the weather may be cold and dreary, but beyond this bibbed photograph of baby Gabriela, which Iris has hung as a kind of totem, is an apartment filled with the warm spirit of new beginnings.

Gazing calmly from her father's lap, Gabriela is right at home and in complete control of the situation.

While pregnant, Iris researched and wrote a book on the immigration experience of women.

ful," she says, handing Gabriela to Philip as a small cadre of volunteers begin moving furniture, laying out multicolored table cloths, blowing up balloons, hanging crepe paper, and lining the buffet table with small wooden animals. Gazing calmly from her father's lap, Gabriela herself seems right at home and in complete control. When she threatens to fuss, her father offers a finger to suck and she immediately calms again. Philip blushes at his fatherly success, though he's completely in her sway.

Gabriela *is* beautiful. With a full head of dark hair, penetrating eyes, a petite, perfectly shaped face, she could easily pass for a newborn fairy tale princess. Traces of her Greek, Jewish, and Hispanic ancestry add to her beauty. Around her tiny neck hangs a necklace with a delicate pendant of the Madonna and child, a gift from her maternal grandmother, Irys Gomez. Irys is a quiet woman, shy about her imperfect English; she emigrated from Columbia in the 1950s.

Iris, inspired in no small part by her mother's experience, is now a lawyer specializing in immigration rights. She is also a serious poet. An unusual combination, hers, but Iris has always had a knack for integrating the different facets of her life. Shortly before becoming pregnant with Gabriela, she took a leave from her legal career to research and write a book on the immigration experience of women in America.

If Iris has had a less than conventional professional life, she and Philip, himself the product of the unusual union of a Greek Orthodox mother and Jewish father, have never had an exactly conventional relationship, either. They met in Boston in 1978. Three years later, Philip, like Iris a lawyer with a strong social conscience, moved to Washington State to run a legal services office. Iris moved out west two months later, but her own legal work pulled her back to Boston in 1984. In 1986, after spending their savings on a large wedding and a honeymoon exploring Africa, they turned their transcontinental romance into a transcontinental marriage until Philip returned to Boston two years later.

As Philip is the first to acknowledge, "We've had lots of ups and downs. When we got married in Miami, if there had been a poll taken, most people would have been iffy on whether we'd still be together five years later. The fact that we're a couple of free and independent spirits and that, nonetheless, Gabriela

has arrived in our lives makes us special to people."

The way they have chosen to commemorate Gabriela's arrival in their lives typifies their unorthodox approach to life. Most celebrations of birth—christenings, brits, baptisms—have a formal religious significance that Iris and Philip wanted to avoid. Instead, they have fashioned a welcoming for their daughter that emphasizes the humanistic values they share as well as their strong sense of family and community.

Community—people who care deeply about each other—has always been an essential part of Iris and Philip's lives. Gently rocking the baby in his arms, Philip credits Iris. "People love Iris because she's got a way of letting them know how much

The eldest of three generations of strong Gomez women, Grandma Irys is soft-spoken; but the portrait hanging on her daughter's wall captures her fiery beauty as a young woman, as well as the strength it must have taken to raise four children after emigrating from Columbia in the 1950s.

The firstborn is a new wonder for this "couple of free and independent spirits."

Guardian Spirits

THE ELATION PARENTS FEEL AT THE MOMENT OF BIRTH ALWAYS CONTAINS AN UNDERCURRENT OF DEEP FEAR. NOTHING IS MORE PERFECT YET SEEMINGLY MORE HELPLESS THAN A NEWBORN CHILD. OUR ANCESTORS FEARED THEIR CHILDREN'S VULNERABILITY TO EVIL SPIRITS AND IN VARIOUS WAYS SOUGHT TO PROTECT THEM. IN MANY CULTURES A TREE WAS PLANTED AT EACH CHILD'S BIRTH TO BE TENDED CAREFULLY, ITS SUCCESSFUL GROWTH TIED TO THE CHILD'S. THE ANCIENT GREEKS BELIEVED THAT EVERY NEW LIFE HAS A PERSONAL PROTECTIVE SPIRIT, A DAEMON, THAT APPEARS AT BIRTH AND WATCHES OVER THE INDIVIDUAL FOR THE REST OF HIS TIME ON EARTH. ∽ THIS SPIRIT, CALLED GENIUS BY THE ROMANS, BECAME THE GUARDIAN ANGELS AND FAIRY GODMOTHERS OF MEDIEVAL FAIRY TALES WHO BRING THE NEWBORN GIFTS AND FORETELL THE INFANT'S DESTINY. CONTEMPORARY RELIGIOUS CEREMONIES OF NAMING AND WELCOMING INTO THE FAITH HAVE EVOLVED FROM THE MEDIEVAL NEED TO GUARD THE INFANT AGAINST HARM. ACCORDING TO EARLY CHRISTIAN LORE, EVIL SPIRITS WERE ESPECIALLY DANGEROUS BEFORE BAPTISM; WITCHES USED THE FAT OF UNBAPTIZED BABIES TO MAKE POTIONS, AND EVIL FAIRIES COULD SWITCH THE INFANTS WITH CHANGELINGS. IN THE JEWISH RITES OF CIRCUMCISION AND NAMING, CALLED THE BRIT, BABIES WERE PLACED ON A SPECIAL CHAIR (NOW CALLED THE CHAIR OF ELIJAH); THERE A GUARDIAN ANGEL WOULD WARD OFF EVIL SPIRITS AND POTENTIAL ATTACKERS. ∽ TODAY GUARDIAN ANGELS HAVE TAKEN HUMAN FORM. WHILE IN SOME PROTESTANT CHURCHES THE ENTIRE CONGREGATION ASSUMES RESPONSIBILITY FOR NURTURING, IN OTHERS AND IN CATHOLIC CHURCHES, SPECIFIC GODPARENTS ARE NAMED. IN GREECE, GODPARENTS ARE RESPONSIBLE FOR THE NAMING CEREMONY, BUYING THE INFANT A WHITE DRESS AND A CROSS TO WEAR, DIPPING THE CHILD IN THE FONT, AND GIVING THE CHILD A NAME. THE HISPANIC TRADITION OF COMADRE AND COMPADRE BONDS THE GODPARENTS EVEN MORE TIGHTLY. SHARING THE JOYS AND PROBLEMS OF THE FAMILY'S DAILY LIFE, EVEN TAKING ON FINANCIAL RESPONSIBILITY IF NECESSARY, THE COMPADRE AND COMADRE BECOME PART OF THE FAMILY BOTH PRACTICALLY AND SPIRITUALLY.

she cares about them and they reciprocate." For her part, Iris credits circumstances. "Part of it has been moving back and forth, meeting different people wearing my different hats through my legal work, my writing, my political volunteer work." She pauses. "I've been lucky to cultivate really wonderful women friends, so instead of replacing, I keep adding friends I cherish and value."

Thanks to those friends, Gilda Gussin, who did most of the physical organizing because she lives nearby, found assigning tasks an easy chore. Lynn Cherry, a children's book illustrator, created the invitations as her gift because she lives too far away to welcome Gabriela in person. Other people willingly took responsibility for decorating the apartment; for bringing the plates, silverware, and a big coffee maker; for picking up and delivering extra chairs; and, most important to new parents getting minimal sleep, for cleaning up afterwards.

"I have loved being involved," Gilda acknowledges as she arranges brightly colored plates and napkins on the serving table. Her friendship with Philip and Iris grew deeper during the pregnancy. "Iris naturally wanted to talk about it a lot, and remembering how anxious I had been when I was pregnant, I understood. I wanted to take care of her." The mother of a two-year-old and contemplating a second child, Gilda loves the idea of a welcoming celebration that connects directly to the parents' lives.

The small apartment is soon crowded with more than sixty people. Spanish and English mingle along with less recognizable lilts and accents. Conversations spill from living room and dining room to kitchen. Small children play in the narrow hallway. Meanwhile, Gabriela sleeps in her bassinet by the front windows undisturbed amid the hubbub.

According to the invitation, everyone was to bring "a festive or ethnic dish," and before long, the table is covered with an incredible international display, reflecting a remarkably wide variety of cultural backgrounds. The colors and scents entice the group to taste everything—a forkful from this plate, a spoonful from that bowl—and they empty each platter almost as soon as it appears on the buffet table.

The savory pastry, filled with goat cheese and potatoes and flavored with rosemary, disappears quickly. So does the coconut flan that Flavio Risech has brought to represent his Cuban background. Flavio met Iris and Philip during law school days. "They're wonderful, exceptional!" he declares. "They're not afraid to do things untraditionally. They have always been determined to live their lives their own way. Plus they have a real spark."

Much of the food turns out to be vegetarian, not ascetic health food but ethnic food from the heart. Tahini from Israel complements a Lebanese lentil casserole. In the kitchen, where Hungarian mushroom soup simmers, Julie McCormack fries Irish potato bread in an iron skillet. Here she serves it

Shari Zimble carries in her Orange, Olive, and Anchovy Appetizer.

with honey and applesauce, but at home in Ireland she'd offer only butter and salt. "Famine food," she calls it.

The table holds much more to tease the appetite: feta cheese triangles and Puerto Rican gingerbread; spicy Peruvian potatoes and an antipasto of oranges, olives, and anchovies; sweet potato pie and Chinese stir-fried spaghetti; flapjacks and chocolate bread pudding.

Some of the dishes represented the culture of the cook. Others are simply personal favorites, like the chocolate cake Audrey Zucker brings in from Rosie's, a popular Cambridge bakery.

Guests eat and talk, oohing and aahing over Gabriela along the way, until Philip initiates the ceremonial portion of the evening. Everyone crowds together in the small living room. On the coffee table sits a bowl of clear marbles, beside it a pretty basket holding colored index cards. The marbles, Philip explains, symbolize the worries all new parents share. "Take a worry out of the house and bury it; leave a wish instead," Gilda exhorts the group.

The gathering takes on a magical quality as the bowl is passed. Throughout the rest of the evening, people stop at the table to take away a worry marble, replacing it with a wish they've written on a card.

"Can my little Gabriela stand my singing a capella?" Grandmother Catherine Kassel croons to begin the evening's lullabies.

Philip announces that he and Iris have asked their friends Nancy Kelly and John Wilshire Carrerra to have a special relationship with Gabriela. John and Nancy gladly accept the roles of compadre and comadre, a Hispanic designation broader than the traditional notion of godparents in this country. According to John, who was raised in Peru, the emphasis centers on their relationship with the parents as well as the child.

"We wanted to remove the religious significance and make it more of a personal relationship," Nancy says. "To formalize that they can turn to us in need," John adds.

"That means you get to babysit a lot," someone jokes. Everyone laughs, but no one questions how seriously Iris and Philip take the roles they have given Nancy and John, who have no children of their own. Nancy and John are equally solemn.

"We're very honored to begin this relationship with the baby," John says. "We were already close to Philip and Iris, but this makes us closer. It feels good to be pulled in, to become like a relative." Nancy is almost awestruck. "I just hope that I have a positive affect on her life that lives up to the sense of responsibility I feel."

By now Gabriela is wide awake, as if she knows what is going to happen next. Iris and Philip have asked everyone to bring not only food but a traditional or favorite lullaby to sing live or to play on tape.

Philip's mother, Catherine Kassel, holds her first grandchild close as she sings the Greek lullaby "Naani,"

Lisa Sheehy sings a German lullaby her mother sang to her. Her voice trembles as she begins her solo, but soon everyone joins in.

or "Sleep." Catherine and her husband, Ed, have altered the words slightly, at least in Ed's translation, to fit the occasion. "Can my little Gabriela stand my singing a capella?" Catherine sings. The baby listens and watches her grandmother in rapt attention. "She liked it. I'm so happy!" Catherine crows when she finishes.

Then Philip, standing behind the sofa on which Iris sits with Gabriela, sings to his wife and child. The song he has chosen is a traditional ballad, "Celito Lindo," which he sings in Spanish. At first he is nervous. The notes quiver, he forgets a few words, but the love unabashedly present in his voice and in his eyes is compelling. Everyone joins in on the refrain.

Philip's sister Melissa, a professional jazz singer, dances in place with Gabriela as she croons a jazz standard. Now more and more people begin to take turns. Some of the

The first card Iris reads from the wish basket says it all: "May Gabriela be loved her whole life as much as she is loved tonight."

lullabies sound familiar, but not all. Having reached far back into their childhood memories, Iris and Philip's friends sing to Gabriela in Spanish, German, Yiddish, and Phunjabi, as well as English. Julie McCormack explains how she knows the Connemara cradle song she's chosen. "I learned it in school in Ireland and forgot it until I had my own child. Then I remembered it out of desperation." The lullaby, with its lilting melody, lures people to join in, never mind that most of them have never heard the song before.

Scott Englander has brought his guitar and an original composition.

"When I opened the invitation and it said, 'bring a lullaby,' I was so pleasantly surprised—never having been asked to do that before—that I just sat down and wrote this lullaby. Writing one is easy in a way because you can be much less inhibited."

Gradually the lullabies have the intended affect. Gabriela, who has acquiesced to being passed from singer to singer, falls asleep. Meanwhile, the lullabies have an equally powerful impact on the singers and listeners, a rare moment of spontaneous communion. Understandably, many of the singers' voices tremble with shy nervousness as they begin their

solos, but no one sings alone for long. They sing with a common purpose, celebrating the miracle of birth. Though many are strangers to each other from a hodgepodge of cultures and ways of life, a tight circle of warmth and tenderness forms with the sleeping Gabriela at its center.

Long after midnight, the bowl empty of worry marbles and the baby miraculously still fast asleep, Iris reads the wishes left for Gabriela to keep in her painted box. The first card she unfolds captures it all.

"May Gabriela be loved her whole life as much as she is loved tonight."

Selections from an International Potluck

Spinach and Feta Appetizers

Orange, Olive, and Anchovy Appetizer

Potatoes and Goat Cheese in Pastry

David's Tahini

Hungarian Mushroom Soup

Lebanese Lentil and Rice Casserole

Tzaziki Sauce

Chinese Noodle Salad

Beth's Chocolate Bread Pudding

Flavio's Flan

SPINACH AND FETA APPETIZERS

Philip was not the only one of Greek ancestry to attend the welcoming for his daughter. Murial Heiberger came and brought her special Spanokopita as an offering. Below, a similar recipe omits the tedious folding of the triangular hors d'oeuvres.

    6 ounces fresh spinach, cleaned
      and chopped, with coarse stems
      removed
    3/4 cup unsalted butter, melted
    2 large eggs, lightly beaten
    8 ounces feta cheese
    8 ounces ricotta
    1 tablespoon minced fresh
      oregano
    1 tablespoon minced fresh
      parsley
    1/4 teaspoon salt
    12 sheets filo pastry

Be sure the spinach is well drained and dry. Place in large bowl with 1/4 cup of the butter and all the remaining ingredients except the filo sheets. Blend together well with a large fork or a wooden spoon and set aside.

To assemble the appetizers, be sure to work with only one sheet of dough at a time and keep the remaining dough tightly covered with plastic wrap or a lightly dampened towel. Otherwise, the dough will dry out quickly and become impossible to work with. Place one piece of pastry on a clean work surface and brush completely with melted butter. Place

second piece on top, brush with butter again, and repeat two more times until you have four layers.

Place 1/3 of the filling in a row along one edge of the layered dough. Fold in sides and roll up. Place on an ungreased baking sheet, seam side down. Repeat with remaining dough until you have three rolls ready to bake. Brush again with melted butter. At this point you may store overnight in the refrigerator or bake in a preheated 375° oven for 18–20 minutes until golden brown. Place rolls on a serving dish and let stand 15 minutes. Slice into 1/2 inch slices with a serrated knife. The rolls may be reheated at 350° in about 10–12 minutes.
Makes about 35–40 slices.

VARIATION: To make individual "bundles," use a sharp knife or pizza cutter and cut each four-layered sheet into 16 squares. Place a half tablespoon of the filling in the center of each, gather the four corners together, and twist. Bake on sheetpan for 15 minutes at 375° in a preheated oven and serve hot.
Makes 48 bundles.

POTATOES AND GOAT CHEESE IN PASTRY

Susan Brooks, another guest at the welcoming, likes this recipe she found in a magazine because it's easy to assemble and appears enticing no matter what free-form shape it takes on. It makes a beautiful and savory addition to

any buffet and is very easy to serve. You might also try the filling in your favorite casserole dish without a crust.

FILLING
    2 1/2 pounds Idaho or Russet
      potatoes
    2 cups milk
    2 cups water
    1 bay leaf
    5 ounces goat cheese, plain
    salt and pepper
    2 tablespoons fresh rosemary
      (or 3/4 tablespoon dried)
    2 tablespoons butter, melted
    1/2–1 cup heavy cream

PASTRY
    2 1/4 cups flour
    pinch of salt
    1/2 cup butter
    1/2 cup shortening
    1 teaspoon wine vinegar
    1/3 cup ice water
    1 egg, lightly beaten

Peel potatoes and slice into 1/4 inch thickness. Place in saucepan with milk, water, and bay leaf. Cook uncovered over medium heat until tender—about 20–25 minutes. Set aside and cool.

To make pastry, place flour, salt, butter, and shortening in a mixing bowl. Using a pastry blender, your fingers, or two knives, cut shortening and butter into flour and salt until a coarse, even texture develops. Stir together wine vinegar and ice water and, mixing with a fork, add the liquids to the flour. Form the mass into a ball of dough. Roll the dough out on a floured surface

to approximately 16 inches in diameter.

To assemble: Brush beaten egg onto the surface of the rolled-out pastry. Using a slotted spoon, remove potatoes from cooking liquid and layer potatoes, goat cheese, and seasonings in the center of the pastry. Drizzle with melted butter and cream. Quickly fold pastry sides up and over some of the potatoes (you won't cover them all). Brush pastry with the remaining egg and bake 1 hour in a preheated 375° oven on a cookie sheet. Remove to a serving platter.

Serves 8–10.

ORANGE, OLIVE, AND ANCHOVY APPETIZER

This is an unusual recipe of Italian origin that is light, refreshing, visually appealing, and easy to prepare. It can be used as a salad or antipasto.

    4 oranges
    1 small tin anchovies
    juice and rind of 1 lemon
    1/4 cup oil-cured black olives

Peel and slice oranges into 1/4 inch slices. Place on platter. Arrange anchovy filets over the top and scatter olives decoratively. Sprinkle with lemon juice and grated lemon rind. Cover and serve chilled or at room temperature.

Serves 8–10 as one of several appetizers.

Potatoes and Goat Cheese in Pastry

DAVID'S TAHINI

David Yavin, himself a new father, is an Israeli studying mathematics in Massachusetts. This was his contribution to Gabriela's welcoming.

16 ounces sesame paste (tahini)
1 cup lemon juice
3/4 cup water
2 medium cloves of garlic, minced
1/2 teaspoon cumin
2 teaspoons salt
freshly ground pepper
1/2 teaspoon paprika
1/4 cup minced parsley

Place sesame paste with its oil (it usually separates) in a large bowl. Using a wooden spoon or an electric mixer, chop up and blend solid portions of sesame paste in oil until smooth. A food processor works well for this. Gradually mix in liquids, continuing until the mixture becomes more homogeneous and forms a smooth paste that gradually falls from the spoon. Add seasonings and serve with pita bread, crudités, or falafel balls.
Makes 4 cups.

HUNGARIAN MUSHROOM SOUP

The kitchen stove where Rhonda Berkower stirred the steaming pot of soup she brought to reflect her Hungarian ancestry was a popular gathering spot for guests as they arrived on a chilly January night. This recipe was inspired by that rich and satisfying soup.

1/4 pound bacon, chopped
1 large onion, chopped coarsely
1 pound mushrooms, rinsed and sliced
1 tablespoon dill
1/2 teaspoon nutmeg
2 teaspoons paprika
salt and pepper to taste
6 cups chicken stock
1–1 1/2 cups sour cream, or to taste

Sauté bacon in a saucepan until soft and translucent, then add onions and mushrooms. Continue cooking until mushrooms are cooked through. Add seasonings and stock and simmer for 15 minutes. Stir in sour cream to taste. Serve hot.
Serves 8–10.

LEBANESE LENTIL AND RICE CASSEROLE

Jeff Boshar's recipe comes from his well-used Gourmet Cooking from Syria and Lebanon, a church cookbook published by St. George's Church Guild in Lawrence, Mass. We have added more seasoning to the dish and cook it in stock instead of water. We recommend serving the casserole with the Tzaziki Sauce that follows. The casserole provides a perfect meatless protein and is inexpensive enough to feed the multitudes.

1 cup dried lentils
2 1/2 cups chicken stock
1 small onion, diced
1/2 teaspoon cumin
1/2 teaspoon coriander
salt and pepper
1/3 cup washed rice
1 large onion, sliced
1/4 cup olive oil

Rinse lentils in a colander and place in a pot. Add 2 1/2 cups of stock or water, cover, and boil 10 minutes. Add diced onion, seasonings, and rice. Stir together, cover, and cook the mixture over low heat another 15 minutes.

Meanwhile, sauté the sliced onion in olive oil until well browned. When the casserole mixture is done, remove to serving dish or reheatable casserole and pour onion and oil mixture over the top. Serve hot or at room temperature.
Serves 6–8.

TZAZIKI SAUCE

1 clove garlic, minced
1 cup plain yogurt
1 cup chopped cucumber
1/2 teaspoon salt
1 teaspoon wine vinegar

Blend together ingredients and refrigerate several hours before serving. Serve with Jeff's Lentil and Rice Casserole, either on top or to the side. It is also excellent inside sliced pita bread with vegetables or atop roasted lamb as a relish.

CHINESE NOODLE SALAD

This dish was inspired by the several stir-fried dishes at Gabriela's dinner. As a buffet dish, it holds beautifully for hours and adds crunch and color to the selection.

6 ounces green beans
6 ounces broccoli
6 ounces snow peas
4 ounces bean sprouts
1 red bell pepper
1 8-ounce can water chestnuts
1/2 cup chopped scallions
1/4 cup julienned fresh ginger
3 tablespoons minced garlic
1/2 teaspoon red pepper flakes
1/2 teaspoon chili paste
1 tablespoon honey
3/4 cup soy sauce
1/4 cup rice vinegar
1 1/2 tablespoons toasted sesame
  oil
1/2 cup peanut oil
12 ounces spaghetti

Snap the ends of the green beans and cut into two-inch pieces. Cut woody stems off broccoli and break flowerettes into 1 1/2 inch pieces. Remove ends and strings from snowpeas. Remove any wilted stems from the sprouts. Steam or blanch the prepared vegetables separately until brightly colored and tender, but still a little crispy to the bite. Place in colander and run under cold water to stop them from cooking. Drain and set aside. Slice red pepper into julienne strips and mix together with the scallions, drained water chestnuts, and cooked vegetables in a large bowl.

Prepare sauce: Heat 2 teaspoons of the oil in a small skillet and add the ginger, garlic, and red pepper flakes. Sauté briefly and remove from heat. Combine with the honey, soy sauce, rice vinegar, sesame oil, chili paste, and peanut oil. Set aside.

Cook spaghetti according to package directions, making sure not to overcook. Drain and rinse with cold water. Toss together all the ingredients together in a large serving bowl. Serve immediately or store several hours. Be sure to toss again before serving cold or at room temperature.
Serves 6–8 as a main entrée.

CHOCOLATE BREAD PUDDING

This is Beth Stickney's adaptation of a recipe she used many years ago and misplaced. It's hard to imagine a bread pudding richer than this one. Guests at the welcoming crowded around the empty dish searching for one last lick from the pan.

8 ounces french baguette, sliced
  in 1/4 inch slices
3 cups heavy cream
1 cup whole milk
8 egg yolks
2 whole eggs
1/2 cup sugar
1 tablespoon vanilla
1/2 teaspoon cinnamon (optional)
10 ounces semi-sweet chocolate
2 ounces bitter chocolate
1/4 cup rum (optional)
whipped cream

Place sliced bread on a cookie sheet and let dry for a day or in a 250° oven for about 2 hours. Line the bottom of an oven-proof casserole dish with the bread slices and continue stacking until all are in the dish.

In a heavy-bottomed saucepan, heat cream and milk until just warm. Whisk eggs together with the sugar and vanilla and blend with the cream. Melt chocolate in top half of double boiler and gradually whisk into egg-cream mixture. Add the optional cinnamon and rum. Pour chocolate custard over the bread and let stand a minimum of 45 minutes to be sure it soaks well into the bread. Occasionally push bread into mixture or turn over slices to aid the soaking process.

Place pudding in a shallow pan of warm water (bain-marie) in a preheated 350° oven for 1 hour or until knife inserted in the center comes out clean. Serve warm with whipped cream.
Serves 10–12.

VARIATION: If cholesterol is a concern for you or your guests, we recommend that you skip this dessert altogether. A second choice would be to substitute half and half and skim milk for the cream and whole milk. Then use 4 egg yolks and a package of egg substitutes instead of the 8 egg yolks and whole eggs.

FLAVIO'S FLAN

Flavio Risech brought his own special version of the classic Cuban flan that included coconut. This is a very simple recipe to reproduce and serve on a buffet. You may even make it in a serving casserole for easy presentation and storage.

3/4 cup sugar
2 cups sweetened shredded
   coconut
2 14-ounce cans sweetened
   evaporated milk
1 cup water
6 large eggs
1 teaspoon vanilla
1/4 teaspoon salt

Preheat oven to 350°. Caramelize the sugar by placing it in a heavy-bottomed skillet over low heat. Stir slowly as the sugar melts and darkens in color. Pour caramel into a 1 1/2 quart casserole or a standard loaf pan, spreading it around to cover the bottom and sides. Set aside.

Mix together remaining ingredients in a bowl with a whisk until blended evenly. Pour the custard into the prepared pan. Make a bain-marie (water bath) by placing flan pan inside another larger pan and filling the larger pan with very hot water that comes within an inch of the top of the flan pan. Very carefully, place both pans in the lower third of the oven and bake for 35–40 minutes, or until a knife inserted in the center of the flan come out clean. Since the coconut has a tendency to rise to the top of the flan and browns more quickly, the color may be a little browner than other flans.

Chill before serving. If you wish to unmold the flan, loosen it with a knife around the edges first, then invert onto your serving dish. Spoon caramel sauce over and around it. If the caramel has hardened on the pan, break off pieces and place on the flan.
Serves 8–10.

Chocolate Bread Pudding

After spending every day for two weeks baking in Glenda's kitchen, Lucy Smith still finds the energy to stir a pot of her special Milanese gravy, a pot so huge she must stir it with a boat paddle.

St. Joseph's Day: A Festival of Food & Faith in New Orleans

Glenda Lubrano loves the Sicilian tradition of St. Joseph. Not that she's Sicilian herself. She's not even Italian. She is a devout Catholic, however, and has been married for thirty-one years to the grandson of Sicilian immigrants. Besides, who could quibble once they've witnessed Glenda's enthusiasm for Sicily's patron saint? Once Glenda catches you up in her whirlwind of baking and decorating, once you gaze into the glow of votive candles on her overflowing altar, once you taste the fig cookies and biscotti she presses on everyone who stops by, you begin to wonder if you could become Sicilian, too, at least every St. Joseph's Day.

On a Saturday afternoon four days before Glenda's St. Joseph Day altar is scheduled to open for public viewing, the Lubrano household is a cheerful madhouse. Platters, some empty, some piled with pastel cookies, cover every surface. Doorbells and telephones ring constantly. Children and dogs play happily. And thirteen women, ranging from Glenda's eighty-one-year-old mother, Althea, to her youngest daughter, seventeen-year-old Margaret, crowd into Glenda's modest kitchen as they have daily for the last two weeks. They are baking cookies—dozens and dozens of seed cakes, anise cookies, yeast balls, cocoons, and biscotti.

"How do you like my hired help?" Glenda asks with her trademark crooked smile. Glenda's friends are used to being enlisted for Glenda's endless volunteer projects. These thirteen are just a sampling from the network of men and women who serve, cook, and clean up annually at the Lubranos' altar. Many of the women are Italian, but not all. Glenda jokes, "One of my friends told me she is definitely going to heaven. She's a Methodist married to a Jew and helping me with St. Joseph's Day."

Today Glenda has everyone making fig cakes. On one side of the table the women use thin wooden rollers to roll out dough in rectangles. Meanwhile, two others shape Glenda's homemade fig paste into sausage-like lengths. Further down the table, several others wrap the dough around the fig mixture, then cut it into two-inch fat logs that are baked until golden. The icing, in pastel colors, comes later.

This cookie making is serious business. Glenda, who has taken advanced courses in baking, will use

Glenda's friends are used to being enlisted for her projects. "If any of us gets a divorce it's Glenda's fault because we're never home," they kid.

Four days before the altar opens, the fig-cake assembly line is in full swing in Glenda Lubrano's kitchen.

350 pounds of flour by the time the altar is ready. The mood, however, is far from serious. "Why do men die first?" one woman asks rhetorically as she rolls the fig paste between her palms. "Because God gives us a break." The women roar with laughter.

Glenda is everywhere, at the table rolling dough, checking the oven, pouring diet soda, talking on the phone, feeding the cat. Not only is she building and decorating the altar for St. Joseph's Day this week; in her spare time she is sewing a wedding dress for a friend's daughter and organizing a talent show for handicapped children at her daughter Glennie's school.

"I've learned to make friends with my dustballs," Glenda says, explaining why vacuuming, waxing, and polishing always take a back seat to what she considers higher priorities

When Glenda built her first altar in 1984, she pledged to build one every year, a pledge she intends to keep.

in her crowded schedule.

And the St. Joseph's altar is a high priority for Glenda, a concrete way to express her firm belief in and gratitude to St. Joseph for her life's blessings. A devout woman, Glenda built her first St. Joseph's altar in 1984 after her husband, Mike, had surprised her with a trip to the religious shrine at Fatima, Portugal. "I'd always wanted to do an altar because we've been very fortunate," she says, pointing to her six daughters and one son. "When I got back from that trip, I said we had to." She's done one ever since.

There are strong traditions in setting up a St. Joseph's altar. First, in recognition that St. Joseph has interceded in your life, you are expected to make a pledge to continue the altar yearly. That commitment was no problem for Glenda, who believes "no matter how big your problems are, if you make a promise you've got to follow through unless you're dead." Second, you must beg for supplies, buying as little as possible. Her first year, Glenda called seventy friends, told them she was building a St. Joseph altar, and asked what they would donate. "I needed everything," she remembers, laughing. Glenda is not the kind of woman you turn down. "Sixty donated up front and the others all showed up and brought stuff."

But there remained the small problem of recipes for the special cookies that traditionally appear on the St. Joseph altar. "In this town no one will give you recipes. The first year I spent my husband's bonus from his job on several hundred dollars' worth

One rule in setting up an altar is to beg for supplies, and Glenda's friends are always generous. One friend even sends live lobsters from his home in Boston every year.

The Origins of St. Joseph's Day

THE STORY HAS BEEN HANDED DOWN FOR CENTURIES: LONG AGO, A SEVERE DROUGHT STRUCK SICILY, KILLING ALL THE CROPS. THE PEOPLE WERE STARVING. ALL THEY COULD GROW TO EAT WERE LITTLE GREEN FAVA BEANS. SO THE SICILIANS PRAYED TO THEIR PATRON SAINT ST. JOSEPH, PROTECTOR OF THE FAMILY, AND HE ANSWERED THEIR PRAYERS BY SENDING RAIN AND AN ABUNDANT HARVEST TO END THE FAMINE. ∽ TO THANK AND HONOR ST. JOSEPH, THE SICILIANS BUILT ALTARS OF FOOD AND GAVE IT AWAY TO THE LESS FORTUNATE. THUS BEGAN A TRADITION. EACH MARCH 19, ALL ACROSS THE ROCKY HILLSIDES OF SICILY, FAMILIES PREPARED ELABORATE HOME ALTARS OF PASTA, PASTRY, AND SEAFOOD. A FEW HUNDRED YEARS LATER, IMMIGRATION TO THE NEW WORLD BEGAN. NEW ORLEANS EMBRACED THE HIGH-SPIRITED, DEVOUT SICILIANS, AND THEIR ST. JOSEPH'S DAY TRADITIONS JOINED THE CITY'S CALENDAR OF CELEBRATION. ∽ FAMILIES WHO HONOR ST. JOSEPH IN THEIR HOME BUILD A THREE-LEVEL ALTAR TO REPRESENT THE HOLY TRINITY. THEY COVER THE ALTAR FROM END TO END WITH PLATES PILED WITH FIG CAKES, A DOZEN VARIETIES OF COOKIES, ELABORATELY ICED CAKES, BREADS BAKED INTO SYMBOLIC SHAPES LIKE JOSEPH'S STAFF, FRESH FRUITS, DELICATE CASSEROLES, WINE, FLOWERS, AND RELIGIOUS STATUES. THOUGH TRADITION DOESN'T DICTATE THAT THE ALTARS BE LARGE, IN NEW ORLEANS THEY TEND TO BE HUGE, SOMETIMES TAKING UP AN ENTIRE ROOM. ALTARS ARE NOT JUST A MATTER OF SHOW; BACKYARDS ARE LINED WITH TABLES WHERE STRANGERS AND FRIENDS ALIKE FEAST ON PASTA, TRADITIONAL SICILIAN VEGETABLES, BREAD, CAKE, COOKIES, AND WINE. ∽ ST. JOSEPH'S PILGRIMS TRY TO VISIT NINE ALTARS. BAY LEAVES ON THE DOOR INDICATE THAT AN ALTAR IS INSIDE. THE NEW ORLEANS *TIMES PICAYUNE* SETS ASIDE SPACE FOR FAMILIES WITH ALTARS TO ANNOUNCE WHAT TIMES THEY'LL BE OPEN. ALTHOUGH NO ONE IS REQUIRED TO PAY TO SEE THE ALTAR OR TO EAT, A BASKET IS USUALLY AVAILABLE FOR DONATIONS TO LOCAL CHARITIES. AND NO ONE IS ALLOWED TO LEAVE EMPTY-HANDED. FAVA BEANS, "FOR LUCK," COOKIES, AND PIECES OF BREAD GO HOME IN A SMALL BAG WITH EACH VISITOR.

For Gina and Sandro Piera, organizing a community altar at the Plaza d'Italia downtown is a family effort. "We do it because we're very blessed," says Gina, "and because we don't want to see it die out."

of cookies. I sent him to the bakery to pick them up without mentioning that I hadn't paid for them."

By her second year preparations became easier. "And much cheaper!" she says with a laugh. In the meantime Glenda had returned to Fatima with her daughter, Glennie, who has Down's syndrome, and a group of handicapped children. After the trip, one of the mothers called to say she'd love to help Glenda with St. Joseph's Day.

Glenda told her she needed recipes, "and she says, 'No problem. I'll bring my cousin Anna.'" Anna Orlando, then in her late seventies, brought Glenda her personal book of recipes. "Once we had the recipes, we were A-OK." Glenda offers a taste of fig cake, warm from the oven. "Of course Anna was from the old school. No short cuts. You mixed three batches in three bowls. Now we know the short cuts. That's why we wait

until the eleventh hour. Remember we have Mardi Gras too at this time of year."

∽

While Glenda and perhaps a hundred other families in the New Orleans area work on the altars in their homes, Gina Piera and her husband, Sandro, plus dozens of volunteers, put the finishing touches on a public outdoor altar that the Greater New Orleans Italian Cultural Society has sponsored for twenty-five years. Although the traditional pasta and bread will not be served until St. Joseph's Day itself, the huge altar downtown at the Plaza d'Italia opens for public viewing three days ahead.

"Initially we got involved because we didn't want to see it die," says Gina, a pediatric nurse of Sicilian descent. Also, like Glenda and most of those who create altars, Gina felt thankful to St. Joseph for her personal good fortune. "We had been childless for ten years," she explains quietly. "We had gone from doctor to doctor. We prayed to St. Joseph. We prayed to everybody. Then I got pregnant with the twins and my due date was St. Joseph's Day."

The downtown altar is both a community and a family effort. "My mom, my aunt, my dad all help," Gina says. "My sister bakes my lamb cakes. Sandro's sister heads up the whole baking project." As for Gina's role, "I'm the head beggar. What I can't get for free, I try to get for a better price."

While Gina hangs decorations and supervises where the breads and intricate filigreed cookies are

placed on the altar, Sandro, a tile and marble contractor born in Italy (Abruzzi, not Sicily), does last-minute carpentry. A red-bearded bear of a man, Sandro exudes quiet good cheer as he mingles with the other volunteers. And, despite some intermittent rain, the volunteers are out in force. Many helping out this Sunday morning after Mass have worked on altars all their lives.

Louise Guerra, eighty, carries on a St. Joseph's Day tradition her mother began. "I was sick as a child, so she burned a candle every year at St. Joseph's Day. That was the promise. Since then I still burn a candle. I get a satisfaction out of helping. I feel that St. Joseph is helping me."

Peter Bertucci, who came to New Orleans in 1949, remembers baking St. Joseph's Day cookies as a small boy in Sicily. "My mother and my aunt and my mother's friends would

Peter Bertucci, who has celebrated St. Joseph's Day since he was a small boy in Sicily, brings a fava bean plant from his backyard garden to the community altar.

Besides all the altars that honor St. Joseph, his statue is in one of the many floats of the St. Joseph's Day Parade.

put up a table and I would help them. I've been making cookies ever since." An avid gardener, he dug up a fava bean plant from his backyard to bring to the Plaza display.

These are dedicated people. Peter's wife, Dolly, broke her arm last week while mixing flour for cookies in the big commercial mixer the society uses. "I didn't faint or anything," she says, brushing off the injury.

Gina, who in addition to her five-year-old twins has a six-month-old baby, acknowledges that sometimes

the work required for St. Joseph's Day is daunting. "I'll be honest with you, my feelings can be mixed. I get stressed out and think, why is this on me? But Sandro and I feel very obligated. We want to educate people about the customs." She pauses. "And it's become more spiritual for me over the years."

Shortly before noon, as if on cue, the cloudy sky clears completely for the opening ceremony. Father James Turrentino lights the candles and blesses the baked goods, fruits, veg-

etables, flowers, candles, and statues. One woman shyly asks him to bless a bag of fava beans so she can hand them out at home. Because fava was the only crop that continued to grow during the famine, it is considered lucky. Many New Orleanians carry one bean around for years.

⁓

Glenda's altar is scheduled to open for viewing at 7:00 P.M. on St. Joseph's eve. Mike has built the three-tiered altar on large sheets of plywood that hide the den couch

A branch of bay leaves on the door invites all passersby to visit the St. Joseph's Day altar inside.

and coffee table underneath. By 5:30, the altar is already crowded with cookies, sculpted breads, and statues. Glenda has to climb onto the altar itself to make room for more dishes. And there are lots more dishes to come—crawfish, artichokes, lobsters that her friend Dennis Schwartz sends live from Boston every year, a cake she has yet to ice, and pignolati cookies a new group of "hired help" is making back in the kitchen.

Meanwhile in the backyard standing at a cauldron-like pot, Lucy Smith uses a boat paddle to stir the Milanese gravy of tomato and anchovies she's made for Glenda since the first year. Lucy has been at Glenda's every day for the last two weeks, and she looks exhausted as she pushes her paddle through the thick sauce. The question comes up, what do these people get in return for all their hard work?

"I don't even know where to start," Glenda responds. "But let me give a quick example." Glenda's quick examples are often mesmerizing yarns. "One year, two of the women I separately invited to help showed up at the same time. It turned out they are first cousins who had not spoken for years, one of those family disagreements. Now here they were side by side baking in my kitchen. At first it was pretty tense in that kitchen. Then they started talking in Italian. I don't speak Italian, but there were certain words I was hearing that I understood and I was getting nervous. The next thing I knew they were laughing. Now they have lunch together once a week."

No feuding cousins are in the kitchen today as preparations shift into high gear. Leaves of bay are hung on the front door to announce the altar inside. As soon as the pignolati are finished, Glenda starts her helpers on the final baking project—delicate muscardini, Italian for the delicate bones they resemble. Meanwhile Mike begins to stuff artichokes, a Lubrano tradition. Although allergic to garlic—"Can you believe I'm Sicilian, allergic to garlic?"—Mike is a skilled cook who at one time marketed his stuffed artichokes to supermarkets nationwide.

He is very supportive of the altar. "I get the satisfaction that I've done something to help other people." He pauses. "Actually, I think St. Joseph's Day is getting bigger and bigger. We're seeing more altars now than we've seen before."

A little after six, Glenda puts out her donation basket. She hopes to raise close to $1,000, none of which will reimburse her own sizeable expenses. All contributions will be divided among the St. Michael's scholarship fund, Covenant House, and Camp Rainbow for disabled kids.

Glenda finds a spot for the cake she has iced to look like an open Bible. She lights the altar candles and makes sure enough lemons are scattered about. Lemons are important, she says. "Single girls are supposed to steal a lemon from the altar

A St. Joseph's Day parade is held on Saturday night. In festive New Orleans tradition, flowers and bead necklaces are tossed from a wild array of floats.

When twelve-year-old Kristen Swearingen sees Glenda's altar for the first time, she is awestruck. "I never thought food could be so beautiful," she says.

Jesus, Mary, Joseph, and two angels—children from a local day-care center—are served a symbolic meal at the Plaza d'Italia before anyone else shares in the pasta and salad that volunteers serve to all who stop by.

and bury it in their yard." She nods discreetly toward an unmarried helper. "Within the year they'll meet the man they'll marry. We laugh, but New Orleans is a superstitious town. I know three that have had it work."

A hush falls over the altar as the first visitors arrive. Twelve-year-old Kristen Swearingen has never seen an altar before. Her eyes grow round as saucers. "This is not what I expected. There is so much. And I love the smell." She points to a shiny loaf of bread shaped into a fish. "I thought that was some kind of statue at first. I never knew that food could be so beautiful."

∞

By 9:30 the next morning Glenda has spread red and white checked cloths on the tables around the pool, where visitors will be invited to eat a light meal after viewing the altar inside. Lucy is stirring two pots, one a container of her Milanese gravy, the other a plain tomato gravy with hard-boiled eggs. Biaggio Di Martino,

Glennie and her classmates participate in a special blessing of the Lubrano altar. According to her older sister Barbara, "Glennie has brought the family closer together through all the activities she's in."

the spaghetti cooker, sets up his butane-fired pot. In the kitchen the morning's volunteers heat vegetable frittatas and toss salad while Glenda's daughters hang Italian flags in the front yard.

Father Densil Perrerra is scheduled to bless the altar a little after noon, but at 11:30 Glennie's class from St. Michael's School arrives to surprise Glennie, at home today to help her mother. Father Perrerra,

Archbishop Phillip Hannan conducts Mass for several hundred gathered at the Plaza d'Italia. Businessmen rub shoulders with homeless men, secretaries with tourists, construction workers with schoolchildren brought in by the busload.

dressed in his robes, thrills the children by leading them in a special blessing. Afterwards, Glenda gives each child a special bag that includes a small St. Joseph medallion along with the usual cookies, bread, and fava beans that all visitors can expect.

∞

At the Plaza d'Italia, Archbishop Phillip Hannan conducts Mass for the several hundred people gath-

At the Plaza d'Italia, "Jesus" gets a hug from his grandma.

ered. Businessmen in suits rub shoulders with homeless men, secretaries chat with tourists, construction workers make room for children bused in from local public schools. The traditional procession is led by children from a local day-care center dressed as Jesus, Mary, Joseph, and two angels. According to custom, the costumed saints are served a symbolic meal. Then Estella Mantia, a native of Sicily who looks like Melina Mercouri and sounds like Sophia Loren, begins to dish up her version of spaghetti with Milanese gravy to all who ask.

She turns no one away. Many are genuinely poor and hungry, not so different from those served at the first St. Joseph Day hundreds of years ago. "You forget about your worries when you look at the expression on the face of these people," she says as she works. "You think, mission accomplished. This is truly beautiful."

∞

Back at the Lubranos', Father Perrerra leads the forty to fifty visitors gathered around the altar in a hymn. He talks about the meaning of St. Joseph's Day, stressing the role of the family and the universal quest for peace, before he offers the formal blessing.

Each visitor who stops by the Lubrano altar instantly becomes a personal guest whom Glenda enthusiastically encourages to come outside for something to eat. Along with Lucy's spaghetti, there are several kinds of frittata and casseroles, salad, cake, iced tea, and wine.

Father Perrerra, who never cele-

brated St. Joseph's Day in his native Sri Lanka, takes an active part, handing out necklaces left over from St. Patrick's celebrations and playing the organ. Everyone is plied with tastes of this, bites of that. The generosity in the air is infectious, especially since similar ceremonies are flourishing at homes, churches, and schools all over the city.

"It is an outward display of people's faith and what they feel they ought to be doing in their community," explains Pat Sharpe, a Presbyterian who met Glenda through the medical profession, as she helps serve pasta to all the new backyard friends. "Even though I'm not Italian or Catholic, I've gone to St. Joseph's altars all my life. After all, as Father Perrerra says, St. Joseph is the Patron Saint not just of Sicilians, not just of Italians, but of the universe."

Father Densil Perrerra never celebrated St. Joseph's Day in his native Sri Lanka, but he gets right in the spirit at the Lubranos' altar, handing out trinkets and playing a mean organ.

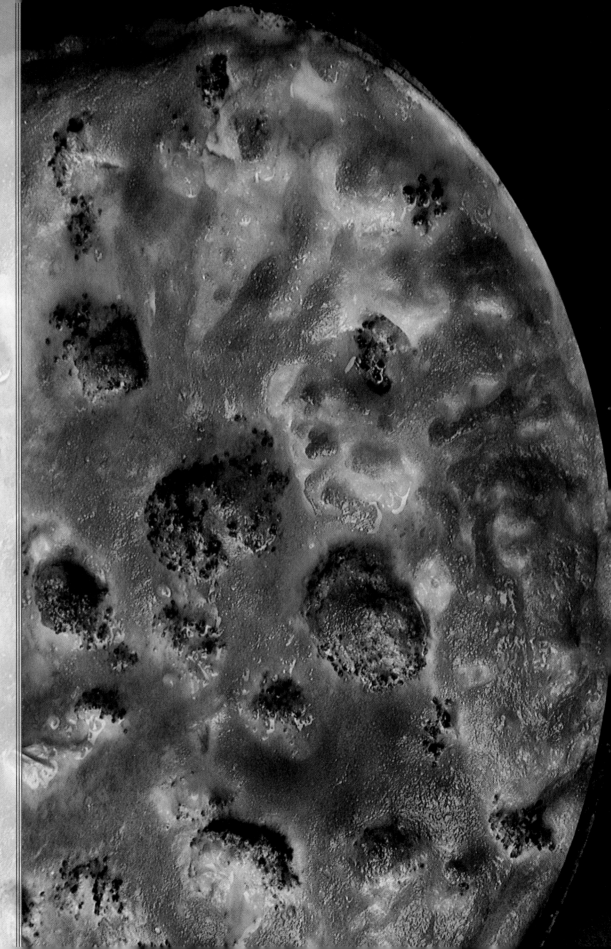

A Sampling of Sicilian Specialties

Mike Lubrano's Stuffed Artichokes

Broccoli Frittata

Macaroni with Milanese Gravy

(Spaghetti with Meatless Tomato Sauce)

Pignolati (Haystacks)

Fig Cakes

Cookie Frosting

Seed Cakes

St. Joseph's Sfinge

Cocoons

Muscardini (Bones)

STUFFED ARTICHOKES

Mike Lubrano used to be in the stuffed artichoke business, and no one else can stuff an artichoke with his speed and finesse. In the recipe below, which he got from his mother, are some helpful hints we observed. The stuffing is enough for at least twelve artichokes, but you can stuff fewer artichokes and freeze the leftover stuffing mixture for future artichokes or use it as a base for stuffing eggplant, zucchini, or meats.

8 ounces grated romano cheese
16 ounces dried breadcrumbs
2 teaspoons salt
3/4 teaspoon black pepper
2 1/2 teaspoons garlic powder or
  4 cloves minced garlic
3/4 cup minced fresh parsley
freshly grated rind of 4 lemons
12 whole artichokes
1/2 cup olive oil
juice of 2 lemons (optional)

Mix together all the above dry ingredients in a large bowl. Cut off ends (bottom and top) of each artichoke and spread the leaves apart with your fingers. Holding each artichoke over the bowl with the breadcrumb mixture, sprinkle the mixture generously into the artichoke until the stuffing fills the spaces between each leaf. Using a bottle with small holes punched in the top, sprinkle the olive oil mixed with the optional lemon juice over artichokes and into the stuffing to moisten thor-

oughly. Place the artichokes upright on a rack or inverted plate above 1/2 to 1 inch of water. Cover the pan and cook over medium heat for approximately 1 hour and 15 minutes, testing for doneness by pulling out leaves from close to the center. Serve warm or at room temperature. **Makes 12 artichokes.**

Stuffed Artichokes

BROCCOLI FRITTATA

A popular Lenten dish that is both inexpensive and good at room temperature, frittatas are practical and traditional offerings on the St. Joseph altar. Some are filled with cardini, cauliflower, and artichokes; others feature the broccoli as done in the following recipe. You may substitute similar quantities of blanched vegetables for the broccoli in the recipe below to create your own combinations.

1 pound broccoli (Cut off coarse stems and separate into flowrettes, reserving stems for other use. You will have 3 1/2–4 cups broccoli.)
8 large eggs
1 cup grated Parmesan cheese
1/2 teaspoon salt
1/4 teaspoon pepper
1/2 cup heavy cream (optional)
4 tablespoons butter or olive oil

In a large pot, blanch broccoli in boiling water for 3–5 minutes until tender but still firm. Rinse immediately under cold running water to stop the cooking. Drain the broccoli and set aside. In a separate bowl, beat the eggs together with the cheese, salt and pepper, and optional cream (it makes a lighter frittata). Stir in broccoli.

Over medium heat, heat butter or oil until hot but not smoking in a 12-inch oven-proof skillet (an iron frying pan is excellent for this). Pour in frittata batter and turn

down heat to low. Continue cooking until eggs have set and only the top remains uncooked. Place pan under high heat in broiler until cooking of top surface is complete and the frittata begins to brown lightly.

Either serve from the pan or loosen frittata with spatula and remove to serving platter. Cut into wedges or squares to serve. *Serves 6–8.*

MACARONI WITH MILANESE GRAVY

(SPAGHETTI WITH MEATLESS TOMATO SAUCE)

Each family altar we visited had its own version of the Milanese gravy, some sweeter than others, some more highly seasoned with anise or fennel and anchovies. All had "sawdust," a mixture of browned breadcrumbs for sprinkling on top to represent dust from the saw of St. Joseph the carpenter. Here is an adaptation for smaller crowds.

 1/3 cup olive oil
 1/2 cup chopped celery
 1/2 cup chopped bell pepper
 1 cup chopped onions
 1 cup chopped fresh fennel
 1 clove garlic, minced
 2 large (56 oz.) cans tomato
  purée
 8 ounces artichoke hearts,
  quartered
 1/2 cup pitted black olives, Greek
  or other oil cured
 1/2 cup green olives

1/2 cup pignolias (pine nuts)
1/2 cup golden raisins
1 tablespoon sugar
1–2 cups water
1–2 tablespoons anchovy paste
  (optional)
size 10 or smaller spaghetti

In a dutch oven or other heavy-bottomed saucepan, sauté chopped vegetables in olive oil until wilted. Add the remaining ingredients, except for the anchovies, and water to thin. Simmer for 1 to 2 hours. Add the optional anchovy paste and simmer another 30 minutes. Serve over "macaroni" (size 10 or smaller spaghetti).
Serves 10–12.

PIGNOLATI (HAYSTACKS)

This is one of the more time-consuming recipes for traditional St. Joseph's Day delicacies, but one that Glenda insists is a "must" for proper observances. Many stories are associated with the symbol of pignolati on the table, some explaining that the confections, shaped like haystacks, remind us of the manger where the baby Jesus was born. Others liken their appearance to the "pinecones" that the Jesus played with as a child. For whichever reason you choose to make them, pray for dry, cool weather to help the caramel work its magic in sticking together the fried dough pieces.

1 1/2 pounds self-rising flour
3 large eggs, beaten
3 cups sugar
3–4 cups oil for frying

Place the flour in a mixing bowl and make a well in the center. Pour in beaten eggs and mix together with a fork. The dough will be stiff. Roll the dough with your hands on a floured surface into pencil-thin strips. With a sharp knife, cut strips into pieces about 1/3 to 1/2 inch long. Meanwhile, heat cooking oil in a fryer or a heavy-bottomed sauce pan. Drop the dough pieces a handful at a time into the hot oil. Remove when lightly browned (1–2 minutes) with a slotted spoon and drain on paper towels. Set aside to cool, then store in a covered container at room temperature until ready to coat with caramel.

  To make the caramel coating, place the sugar in a heavy frying

Preparing the pignolati, or "haystacks," is hard work. After rolling a pan of small fried-dough balls in a hot caramel coating, the women mound them into the miniature haystacks they are supposed to resemble. Burnt fingers are unavoidable.

Cookies, cookies, cookies!

pan, such as an iron skillet, and place over medium heat. Stirring constantly with a wooden spoon, melt the sugar and cook until it takes on a rich brown color and begins to form long golden threads when the spoon is lifted from the pan. Carefully drop in a portion of the fried dough balls, and stir them into the caramel. Take extra care not to splash the caramel as it is very sticky and very hot.

To form into haystacks or other clusters, pour sticky mass onto prepared marble or other smooth and heatproof surface that has been sprayed lightly with nonstick spray. Working quickly before the caramel hardens, use knives or spatulas to separate the pieces and pack some into funnels that have also been sprayed. Invert funnels on work surface and leave the "haystack" to dry while you re-use the funnel to shape another mound. Store in cool dry place in a tightly covered container. **Makes 10–12 pieces.**

FIG CAKES

This has to be the original Fig Newton—only better! The cookies are time consuming but well worth the effort, and they keep well in sealed containers in a cool dry place. In St. Joseph's observances the stuffed dough takes on many artistic shapes and religious symbols, and the tops are often decorated with colorful icings. This recipe is adapted from Trudy Stephens,

who shared it with Glenda Lubrano.

FILLING
1 pound dried figs (with stems removed)
1/4 pound pitted dates
1/2 pound pecans
8 ounces seedless raisins
1/2 orange (grated rind and juice)
1/2 teaspoon allspice
1/2 teaspoon cinnamon
1/3 cup honey
1/8 cup sugar

DOUGH
4 1/2 cups flour
3/4 cup sugar
1 tablespoon baking powder
1/2 cup shortening
2 eggs
1/2 teaspoon vanilla
1/4 cup milk

To make the filling, cut each fig into 3 or 4 pieces. Using either a meat grinder or a food processor, grind or process all solid ingredients into a coarse paste. Don't overprocess— the idea is to retain a chewy texture. Transfer the mixture to a large bowl or mixer and blend together with the remaining spices, honey, and sugar. Set aside or refrigerate until ready to use.

To make the dough, combine the flour, sugar, and baking powder in a bowl. Cut in the shortening with a pastry blender until mixture resembles coarse corn meal. Beat in the beaten eggs and vanilla. Add sufficient milk to hold the mixture together and make a stiff dough.

Pinch off small pieces of the dough and roll them on a floured

surface until they are about 1 inch wide and about 6 inches long. Roll out as thin as possible. Roll filling into pencil-thin logs and place down the center. Overlap dough to seal long seam. (You can leave the ends open or seal them.) Cut the filled strip into three lengths, which you may shape into the customary "s" shapes or leave as "palms," which represent the palms laid in the path of Jesus on his Triumphal Entry into Jerusalem. (At the Lubranos, they snipped the ends to look like palms.) Bake in a preheated oven at 400° for 10–12 minutes. Don't let dough darken.
Makes about 100 cookies.

COOKIE FROSTING

Almost any simple frosting that "sets" to a hard finish will work. Here is an icing that can be tinted to the colors of your choice and will hold up well for long periods at room temperature.

2 cups confectioner's sugar, sifted
2 tablespoons water
1/4 teaspoon vanilla
selection of food coloring
nonpareils (candy beads)

Place confectioner's sugar in mixing bowl and gradually add water while mixing with a fork. Use only enough water to achieve a nice spreading consistency that is not too runny. Add vanilla and blend. Divide the frosting into batches and tint to desired shades with food coloring. Spread frosting over tops of baked cookies and sprinkle with beads. **Makes about 1 1/2 cups.**

SEED CAKES

The sesame seeds in these cookies give them a savory, nutty flavor. They are reminiscent of some commercially prepared "wine biscuits" and make a handy hors d'oeuvre as well as a teatime treat. This recipe is adapted from Glenda Lubrano's recipe, which she got from Rosemary Gennary and Sadie Fortunato, two of her most loyal helpers.

> 1 1/4 cups sugar
> 5 cups self-rising flour
> 1 cup solid vegetable shortening
> 4 eggs
> 1 1/2 teaspoons vanilla
> 3/4 cup sesame seeds

Mix sugar and flour together in a mixing bowl. Cut in the shortening with a pastry blender. Beat the eggs and vanilla in a separate bowl and add to the flour mixture. Mix together well with a large wooden spoon and then knead together briefly with your hands. The dough will be stiff.

Put sesame seeds in a clean, dry dish towel and wash briefly under cold running water. Wring out excess water.

Break off pieces of dough and roll with hands into desired shape (about 1/2 inch wide by 1 1/2 inches long is the traditional shape). Roll biscuits in wet seeds and place on baking pans that are lined with baking parchment. Bake in a preheated oven at 350° for about 20 minutes until the cookies are lightly browned. **Makes 9 dozen.**

ST. JOSEPH'S SFINGE

Countless ethnic groups have their own version of "fried dough," and Sicilians are no exception. This fried pastry is another beloved dish served at altar celebrations. When filled with a pastry cream, it is reminiscent of the Zeppole popular in northeastern St. Joseph's gatherings. This recipe is adapted from Jeannie Alello's recipe printed in the Baton Rouge State-Times in 1979.

DOUGH

> 2 cups flour
> 1 teaspoon baking powder
> 1/3 cup sugar
> 1 or 2 eggs
> 1 cup milk (or more if needed)
> cooking oil
> confectioner's sugar

PASTRY CREAM

> 2 egg yolks
> 1/4 cup sugar
> 2 1/2 tablespoons all-purpose
>   flour, sifted
> 2/3 cup milk
> 2 tablespoons amaretto
> 1/2 teaspoon vanilla
> 1/3 cup heavy cream

To make the dough, mix together dry ingredients in a bowl. In a separate bowl, combine sugar, eggs, and milk, then mix with dry ingredients. Heat 2 inches of oil in a fryer or heavy skillet to about 375–400°. Drop teaspoon-sized pieces of the dough in the hot oil. Fry the pastries until golden brown—about 2–3 minutes. Drain and sprinkle with confectioner's sugar or fill, using a pastry bag, with the pastry cream.

To make the pastry cream, place egg yolks and sugar in a mixing bowl and beat with a mixer until light and fluffy. Gradually add the sifted flour and continue beating until blended. Meanwhile scald the milk in a small saucepan. Add the hot milk in a stream while stirring it into the flour and egg mixture. Transfer the pastry cream to a heavy saucepan and boil over moderate heat for 2 minutes, stirring vigorously. Remove from heat. Add flavorings. Strain if lumpy, cover with buttered waxed paper, and let cool.

In a chilled bowl, beat the chilled heavy cream with an electric mixer until it holds stiff peaks. Stir a little of the cream into the cooled pastry cream, then fold in remaining whipped cream. **Makes 3 dozen 1 1/2 inch pastries.**

COCOONS

These melt-in-your-mouth cookies are named for their shape. When rolled in powdered sugar, they resemble cocoons. Glenda Lubrano got this recipe from Trudy Stephens.

1 1/3 stick butter
6 tablespoons sugar
1 1/2 tablespoons vanilla
2 cups all-purpose flour
1 cup chopped pecans
1/2 cup confectioner's sugar

In a mixing bowl, cream together butter, sugar, and vanilla. Add flour and pecans, blending together well. Using about 1 teaspoon of dough, shape dough with your hands into cocoon shapes (for other uses, a ball shape will do). Bake on an ungreased cookie sheet in preheated 350° oven for 18–20 minutes or until light brown. Be careful not to overcook, as the butter will burn easily. Let cool slightly before rolling in powdered sugar.
Makes 3–4 dozen.

MUSCARDINI (BONES)

These cookies are extra crunchy and often produce tops that curl around like hollow bones. The recipe comes from Anna Orlando, the friend who rescued Glenda in time for her second altar with a complete set of recipes and lots of kitchen help.

2 cups all-purpose flour
2 1/4 cups sugar
1/2 teaspoon baking powder
grated rind of 1 orange
1/2 teaspoon yeast
1/2 cup lukewarm water

In a mixing bowl, mix together flour, sugar, baking powder, and orange peel. Make a well in the center of the flour mixture. Dissolve the yeast in the lukewarm water and pour into the well in the flour. Mix together with your hands into a stiff dough. Knead dough, adding more flour if too sticky to handle. Roll pieces of the dough into narrow logs and cut diagonally. Place the cookies on a greased cookie sheet or one covered with baking parchment, at least 2 inches apart because sugar melts and spreads as it is baked. Let the cookies stand overnight before baking. Bake in a preheated 350° oven about 8–10 minutes until brown.
Makes 5 dozen.

Seed Cakes

PASSOVER SEDER: A Feast of Freedom

For thirty-five years Anne and Max Madorsky have prepared Passover Seders with their family in the same house on Belair Drive in Daytona, Florida. Brothers, sisters, sons, daughters, cousins, and friends—some from down the block, others from half way across the United States—return without fail year after year. Together they pray, sing, ask questions, and eat. And together they renew a shared conviction as strong as religious belief—you don't miss Passover at Grandma and Grandpa Madorsky's.

At 11:00 A.M., seven hours before the first blessing, organized pandemonium reigns in the Madorsky kitchen. Anne and her three grown daughters chop and peel at counters half buried under platters and bowls. Teenaged cousins come and go on errands. Well wishers call repeatedly on the telephone. A contingent of fourth cousins arrive from Ohio and don aprons. There is teasing and tasting, lots of hugs and laughter. Especially when someone discovers a pan of chicken that should have been baking hours ago and pops it in the oven.

Serenely ignoring all the fuss, two very small girls intently stir batter for chocolate macaroons. But when Grandpa Max arrives home from the beachfront motel he still manages at age eighty, Amy and Marsha Rothstein drop their long-handled

The Madorsky grandchildren work together to make charoset, a chopped mixture of apples, nuts, and honey.

spoons and rush into his arms. Thickset, with a cherubic twinkle in his eye, Max tries to look stern, but the mutual adoration is unmistakable as he tickles his granddaughters into giggly abandon.

"For as long as I can remember, this has always been a really and truly family effort," Max says, swiping a lick of batter as he glances around the crowded kitchen. "From this size," and he tweaks Amy's cheek, "on up, each child growing up has taught the next."

As if to emphasize his point,

granddaughter Joan Silverstein, a judge's law clerk in Philadelphia, appears in the doorway. "Time to start the charoset factory," she calls out, and cousins scattered all over the house come running.

Every generation of the Madorsky clan has a role in Passover preparation. The job of the Madorsky grandchildren is to make the charoset*, a traditional Passover dish served to remind Seder participants of the Jews' slave labor in Egypt. In Hebrew, *charoset* means "mortar," which the apples and nuts mixed

*The Hebrew terms in this chapter have various English spellings, since all translations from the Hebrew are phonetic.

The Passover Seder "has always been a family effort," Max Madorsky says, swiping a lick from granddaughter Amy's chocolate macaroon batter.

Elaine Silverstein, the oldest of Max and Anne's four kids, admits she cooks "zero during the rest of the year." In her mother's kitchen she's immediately up to her elbows in roasted lamb shanks.

with cinnamon and wine resemble.

As the oldest unmarried grandchild, Joan is in charge. She spreads bowls and choppers on the cement floor of the Madorskys' garage, where much of the food for the Seder feasting is already stored. Then while she supervises the chopping of the nuts, her mother, Elaine, watching fondly from the kitchen step, leads the group in the family's favorite charoset-making song.

Suddenly Elaine stops singing.

"We seem to be missing something," she whispers to Joan.

"What?" the children ask in chorus.

"THE APPLES!"

Not to worry, after a short if frenzied search, the apples are found under a container of salad in the pantry. The charoset assembly line swings back into operation, a little bit of confusion simply part of the fun.

"Mother's house is torn apart when we're here," Elaine, the oldest of Anne and Max's four children, says laughing. A chic advertising executive, Elaine normally is given to designer suits and dramatic jewelry; today she wears an old shirt and jeans. Heading back into the kitchen, she is soon up to her elbows in roasted lamb shank bones. "Mother is the general in the kitchen," Elaine says. "She expects everyone to get in and help."

As she glides between the kitchen and family room, Anne Madorsky looks less like a general than the calm at the eye of a storm, slim, elegant and completely relaxed as she makes suggestions here and there.

"I love preparing the Seder,"

Anne says, her voice full of energy. "This is such a wonderful way for the family to be together. Each of us has our own little specialties. One cooks, one organizes, one sings."

Smiling with family pride, Anne unpacks the collection of Passover plates and matzah covers she and her children have collected from around the world. She kibitzes with her daughters while she sorts linens and takes out the freshly polished silver goblets, each engraved with a child's or grandchild's name.

"This is an accumulation of fifty years," Anne's brother Nate Korash, a retired florist, explains affectionately from across the room where he is busy arranging flowers for the Seder. Since he still lives up north in Detroit, he also contributes the cold-water pike and white fish with which the Madorskys make their traditional first course of gefilte fish.

And no one ever dares to begin setting the giant U-shaped table before Nate's wife, Betty, arrives. "I don't know why they don't; they always change my arrangement anyway," Betty claims in her gravelly voice as she lays out the tableware for the fifty guests expected tonight.

"Honey, your grandmother has enough stuff here for five thousand people," she says to a nephew on the floor who is taking cellophane off candlesticks. For the next three hours Betty and her helpers spread white linen cloths, set out candelabras, count forks and goblets.

Meanwhile, elsewhere in the house, preparations of a more secretive nature are taking place, plans

Nate arranges the flowers every year. Coming to Florida from chilly Detroit, he is also responsible for bringing the cold-water pike necessary to make gefilte fish.

One yearly ritual is unpacking the matzah covers that family members have collected from around the world. "We are all travelers," says Elaine, "and we love to bring back stuff for Passover."

"Each of us has our own little specialties," Anne Madorsky says, displaying her baking gifts on the dessert table.

Rituals of the Seder

THE HOLIDAY OF PASSOVER COMMEMORATES THE JEWS' FLIGHT FROM ENSLAVEMENT IN EGYPT. AT THE HEART OF PASSOVER, THE FEAST OF FREEDOM, ARE TWO NIGHTS OF RITUALIZED FEAST AND CEREMONY CALLED SEDER, WHICH MEANS "ORDER." THE SEDER IS HELD, NOT AT SYNAGOGUE UNDER A RABBI'S GUIDANCE, BUT AT HOME WITH FRIENDS AND FAMILY. ❧ IN MANY WAYS THE PASSOVER CELEBRATION CENTERS ON THE CHILDREN. EARLY IN EACH NIGHT'S SERVICE THE YOUNGEST CHILD ASKS WHY SEDER NIGHT IS DIFFERENT FROM ALL OTHER NIGHTS. THE ANSWER, A STORY OF ENSLAVEMENT AND DELIVERANCE BY GOD, IS DEVELOPED IN THE RECITATIONS FOUND IN THE HAGGADAH, A BOOK CONTAINING THE LITURGY OF THE SEDER SERVICE, WHICH IS LAID AT EACH PARTICIPANT'S PLACE. IN HEBREW *HAGGADAH* MEANS "TO TELL." THE HAGGADAH OFFERS STRAIGHTFORWARD DIREC-TIONS—WHETHER TO PRAY ALOUD OR SILENTLY, WHEN TO TAKE A SIP OF WINE—AND INCLUDES SONGS, PRAYERS, AND COMMENTARY BY THEOLO-GIANS THROUGHOUT THE AGES. ❧ THE SEDER SERVICE LARGELY REVOLVES AROUND SYMBOLIC FOODS. BEFORE IT BEGINS, TRADITIONAL ITEMS ARE PLACED ON A SPECIALLY DECORATED OR HEIRLOOM PLATE. NO LEAVENED BREAD IS EATEN DURING THE SEVEN DAYS OF PASSOVER, TO REPRESENT THE UNLEAVENED BREAD THAT FLEEING JEWS DID NOT HAVE TIME TO LET RISE. ❧ NO TWO SEDERS ARE EVER CARRIED OUT EXACTLY ALIKE. HAGGADAHS VARY, AND INDIVIDUAL FAMILIES CARRY OUT THE RITUALS IN THEIR OWN WAY. HOWEVER, SOME TRA-DITIONS ARE COMMON TO ALL. EVERYONE PRESENT TAKES A TURN READING ALOUD, LAUGHTER AND FUN ARE AS WELCOME AS PRAYER, AND THERE IS ALWAYS PLENTY TO EAT.

for this year's visit from Elijah, the prophet of redemption. The custom of setting out an extra cup of wine for Elijah and opening a door so he can enter is integral to all Seder ceremonies, his visit representing redemption and a spirit of welcome to all who are hungry. Usually only the spirit of Elijah is expected, but at the Madorskys', a living, breathing Elijah actually comes in when the door is opened near the end of the service.

No one remembers exactly how the visits began decades ago, but for years different uncles showed up in basic biblical costumes, usually sheets. Then about ten years ago, Joan, along with her brothers Steven and Matthew, took responsibility for Elijah's visits. They began creating actual scenes and writing scripts in which Elijah's role was taken over by figures from popular culture. Since then, Elijah has surprised the Seder guests by arriving in a variety of personas, from Michael Jackson to Big Bird. "We try to think of characters that will make the kids laugh but are broad enough to make the parents laugh as well," Joan says. "It's been a lot of work but a lot of fun preparing it together."

Part of the rationale for having Elijah visit, aside from the entertainment value it affords at the Seder, has become to involve those between bar mitzvah age and marriage. The formal Passover service focuses on the younger children's active participation—they ask ritual questions and search for the afikomen, a piece of cracker-like

"Having kids makes the experience a little more powerful," says Anne and Max's youngest daughter, Marsha. "You're more cognizant of what's going on, and can instill in them the same togetherness and significance to the holiday that mother has for us."

unleavened bread (matzah) that is hidden as part of the evening's ritual. The older kids often get minimal attention. Orchestrating Elijah gives the teenagers an important role in the Madorsky service.

The Silversteins, all college graduates now, have grown out of the job. "We're passing the torch," Matthew explains. "We feel an obligation to pass responsibility on to the next group."

Allison and William Goldberg along with their cousin Jon Madorsky are ready. "Now I'm really part of Passover in a major way because I get to plan Elijah," Allison says as the old and new guard plot

in hushed tones how to use the costumes that Aunt Marsha, Amy and Whitney's mother, has provided.

"Whoever has small children wants to see the Seder happen and works the hardest," says Sandra Goldberg, explaining the cycle of responsibility as she watches her teenaged children talk to her sister. "When Elaine's children were very young, I did Elijah." She left that role when she outgrew adolescence. "Then when I got married and had William and Allison, I'd come in from Houston about four days ahead of time to work with Mother. Now Marsha has the youngest kids, so she's the one who

As Max begins the service, everyone shares the bittersweet knowledge that this might be the last gathering of the Madorsky clan in Daytona.

Standing before parents, grandparents, aunts, and uncles, the children proudly recite, in Hebrew and English, the question that lies at the heart of every Seder service: "Why is this night different from all other nights?"

says. "For instance, if the vegetables get over cooked, it doesn't matter." She looks around the room full of people she loves. "What matters is now, being together preparing."

∽

At 5:55, quiet rules. Everyone has gone off to rest and change. The cooking is over, the table set. Anne, impeccably dressed for the evening, takes a few moments for herself. She double checks the dessert buffet set up on the dining room table. Displayed are the dozen cakes, all flourless as required for Passover, all baked by Anne over the last two weeks. But looking at her you'd never guess the effort she's put in. She looks amazingly rested—not to mention young—for a woman in her seventies who's been going strong since she began the day boiling eggs at 4:30 this morning.

Slowly the others begin to arrive: Ann and Max's son Martin with his sons Jon and Robert, cousin Ruthie from Cleveland, cousin Ronna from Atlanta, friends who attend every year, other friends who have never been to a Seder before. At the Madorskys' Seder, friends become family, Jew and Gentile sharing the universal message of freedom and generosity central to the Passover tradition.

Elaine's son Steven, who has given up both his charoset and Elijah duties, stands beside his wife, Cathy, whose baby is due the next month. "It's incredibly exciting to think that next year my child will be here with me," he says. "My role is changing, and I'm glad. There is a feeling of growing up as you move

comes in early. Of course, we all stay involved in different ways as our roles change."

Not that Passover is the only chance to get together. For busy professionals, the Madorskys have remained remarkably family centered. Elaine, Sandra, Marsha, and their brother Martin all live with their families in the same complex in Miami. But getting together at Passover is different. "Passover has always been special because Daytona is an inconvenient place to get to yet everybody comes and loves the whole weekend. The Seder itself is almost a backdrop," Sandra

The Seder Plate. A roasted shankbone of lamb represents the ancient Passover sacrifice. Parsley symbolizes the renewal and hope we feel each spring. Horseradish symbolizes the bitterness of the Jews enslaved under the pharaohs and all those enslaved in the world today. Charoset resembles the mortar used by the slaves to build Egyptian edifices. A roasted egg symbolizes life. A bowl of salt water recalls the tears of suffering people.

through your roles. I've taken our Passover very personally. It always sends shivers up my spine."

His reaction to another possible change is mixed. Anne and Max are thinking of selling the house on Belair and moving to Miami to be closer to their children. This might be the last Passover in Daytona. "Not that the family won't gather for Passover in Miami," Steven says, trying to sound upbeat, "but distractions are there. When everybody comes to Daytona, we're in a cocoon. We've had an insulation here that I love."

Just after 7:00, Max, who as the family patriarch leads the Seder service, calls everyone to the table. As he raises his wine glass to begin the Seder service, all those present share the bittersweet knowledge that this may be the last gathering of the Madorsky clan in Daytona.

But before the service formally gets under way, cousin Ronna stands to make a toast to her Uncle Max in honor of his eightieth birthday earlier in the winter. "He is the most generous and loving man to everyone, especially family," she says, before reminiscing about her childhood. "I was a chubby kid, always on a diet, but I could always count on Uncle Max to put something wonderful in my mouth." Max tries not to beam as he leads his friends and family in prayer.

Mary Ann Richards, a friend of Anne who happens to be Presbyterian, follows the service closely. "The story of the flight from Egypt is my story as well," she says. "I'm a Bible scholar. And I love the Seder. Holding a service in the home is more normal, how it all started."

The children stand up before their grandparents and proudly recite, in English and Hebrew, the question at the heart of the service: "Why is this night different from all

"They are the most extraordinary grandparents," Elaine says about Anne and Max. "They are so inclusionary and so involved. You just feel how important family is to them."

other nights?" Max answers by reading the traditional story of the four sons, one wise, one contrary, one simple, and one who does not know how to ask. Each deserves a different answer, he says, and adds his own commentary. "When you get five Jews together, you get six opinions." Then he sounds the theme of every Passover Seder. "We were slaves to Pharaoh in the land of Egypt and God freed us with a mighty hand."

He leads the group in prayers, offers interpretation and commen-

tary, calls on individuals to read aloud from the Haggadah. Everyone takes a turn. "Grandma's really funny because she knows when someone isn't paying attention," Joan says almost conspiratorially. "She warns people when it's getting close to their turn to read." One by one the symbolic foods on the Passover plates are tasted as their significance in the story of the exodus is recounted. The mood is reverent but informal. "After all, we're celebrating a festival of freedom," Elaine says.

As Max reads the list of plagues

that fell upon Egypt, Elaine interrupts to ask, "What is muraine?" the question that someone, according to Madorsky family tradition, asks to needle Max every year. "Cattle disease," he answers, a little gruffly.

"People are continually coming up with questions to challenge Grandpa," Joan confides. "We banter, joke. It's lighthearted. But there is also a tremendous amount of tradition. Judaism has been a big part of the family. My grandmother is very religious. She celebrates all the holidays. She does the Sabbath every week. The rest of us know how important our religion is to the family even if we don't exactly practice it as regularly."

Three quarters of the way through the service comes the break for dinner. Anne and Max rarely change their menu for the two nights of Seder. Since tonight is the first night, plates of gefilte fish are served, followed by matzah ball soup, baked chicken, and this year's green vegetable, asparagus. Tomorrow will offer chopped chicken liver, borscht, and veal roast. Any cake left unfinished the first night always goes into the next night's trifle, but as guests stretch their legs around the dessert table and sample a little honey cake, a little sponge cake, it's apparent that tomorrow's trifle may be small.

The Seder resumes with a prayer of thanks for divine sustenance sung by Marsha, the unofficial family cantor. Soon the moment comes to open the door for Elijah. Who should walk through but Winnie-the-Pooh with Bart Simpson, not your most likely couple. Pooh uses exaggerated sign language to explain to Bart that he wants a sip of wine from Elijah's cup.

In ragged harmony the assembled sing the traditional songs that have closed the Madorsky Seder every year for as long as anyone can remember. Everyone is tired, but also keyed up, hoping to prolong the evening as long as possible, aware of the richness of this family's faith, its history and future.

When the door is opened for Elijah, who should walk through but Bart Simpson and Winnie-the-Pooh. Laughter and levity are important parts of the Seder.

"Passover in Daytona is what the children and grandchildren have always known," Sandra says with a smile, her voice shaky. "But we'll make new traditions. As long as we're all together, that's all that matters."

A Seder Meal

Lena Goldstein became part of the extended Madorsky family Passover celebration when her son, Charles, married Ann and Max Madorsky's daughter, Elaine Silverstein. She shared this recipe with me some years ago on the eve of her ninetieth birthday.

GRAND LENA'S CHOPPED LIVER

For this menu, we have selected items drawn from those the Madorsky family typically serves on either the first or second night of Passover. With the exception of the Flourless Cheesecake and the sour cream sauce, which contains dairy products, the menu meets Jewish dietary guidelines that meat and dairy products not be served together.

  2 large onions, sliced (or 1
    pound)
  2 1/2 tablespoons vegetable oil
  1 pound chicken livers
  1/2 teaspoon cinnamon
  3 hard-boiled eggs, coarsely
    chopped
  1–2 tablespoons mayonnaise
  1/2 teaspoon salt
  1/4 teaspoon pepper

Sauté onions in vegetable oil over medium high heat until lightly browned. Remove onions from the pan and set aside on a plate. Add the chicken livers to the pan and cook them until only lightly pink in the center. Let cool and add cinna-mon. Grind mixture in meat grinder or in batches in the food processor. Take care not to overprocess—you want to keep some of the texture of the liver and onions. Grate the eggs separately, and stir in, reserving some for garnish. Stir in mayonnaise, salt, and pepper. Place the mixture in a bowl or lightly oiled mold and chill. Unmold onto a serving plate, place crackers or matzah around and garnish with reserved chopped egg.
Makes about 2 cups.

BEET BORSCHT

The Madorskys usually reserve their borscht for the second night of Passover. Its rich color and taste make it virtually a meal in itself.

  1 1/2 pounds thinly sliced beef
    flanken or boneless short ribs
  2 cloves garlic, minced
  1 medium onion, chopped
  2 carrots, coarsely chopped
  2 stalks celery, coarsely chopped
  3 pounds fresh beets (2 large
    bunches)
  rind of 1 orange
  salt and pepper
  6 egg yolks
  1/4 cup chopped fresh dill

Rub the beef flanken with minced garlic and place with fresh vegetables (except beets) in roasting pan. Place in preheated 400° oven for 20–30 minutes until beef is browned. Remove the beef and vegetables to a soup pot, scraping up browned cooking residues to add to pot. Cover with water and simmer for 2 hours.

While the soup is simmering, cut off the green tops and root ends of the beets. Peel the beets with a sharp knife and grate them on the largest holes of a grater, or process through the grater attachment of a food processor. After the broth has simmered, strain out the bones and vegetables and return broth to the pot. Add beets and orange rind. Simmer another hour. Check for seasonings, and return any boned pieces of meat from the original stock if desired. To thicken and enrich the soup, beat egg yolks in separate bowl, then add a ladle full of hot soup to the eggs. Beat together and whisk mixture into soup. Do not boil. Add dill and serve immediately with a sprig of dill for garnish.
Makes 10–12 cups of soup.

GEFILTE FISH

"Gefilte" is a Yiddish word meaning stuffed. In Eastern Europe, the ancestral home of many American Jews, gefilte fish was often eaten on the Sabbath because it was without bones, therefore ensuring that you did not have to "work" on the day of rest to bone the fish. While Anne Madorsky typically starts with sixty pounds of raw fish, we've adapted her recipe (which, to our knowledge, has never been written down) to more manageable por-tions.

3 pounds whitefish fillets
2 pounds yellow pike fillets, or
  5 pounds other freshwater lake
  fish
1 large onion
3/4 tablespoon salt
1/4 teaspoon white pepper
1/4 teaspoon black pepper
3 eggs
1 1/2 cups water
1/2 cup matzah meal
1 carrot

STOCK
bones, head, and skin of fish
4 cups water or enough to cover
  fish
1 tablespoon salt
3 sliced carrots
3 diced onions

To make stock, wrap fish skin, head, and bones in cheese cloth. Cover with cold water and add salt, carrots, and onions. Bring to boil on top of the stove and reduce to simmer for 30 minutes. Remove bones, skim surface, and set aside.

To make the fish: while stock simmers, chop fish filets in food processor or by hand. Be sure not to purée the fish if you are using a food processor—a little texture is desirable. Mince onion and carrot. Mix with remaining seasonings, eggs, and water. The mixture should be thick enough to form into egg-shaped rounds; add a little matzah meal to thicken if necessary.

Slide the fish rounds carefully into simmering stock and cook for 2 hours. Watch carefully to prevent sticking or excess heat which will curdle the stock and toughen the fish.

Remove to a pan with a slotted spoon and refrigerate until ready to serve. Garnish with carrot and lettuce and serve with fresh horseradish. **Makes 40–48 gefilte fish appetizers.**

ROASTED CHICKEN WITH APRICOTS

Because all but the briefest last-minute cooking must be done before the start of the lengthy Passover service, the Madorskys have developed recipes that hold well in the oven, are easily reheated, or can be simply served cold. Roasted Chicken with Apricots is our adaptation of a relative newcomer to their table.

10 ounces dried apricots
1 cup white wine
7 pounds chicken pieces (about 1
    1/2 fryers)
1 teaspoon salt
1/2 teaspoon pepper
1 teaspoon thyme
1/2 teaspoon paprika
2 cups onions, cut in chunks
1 cup carrots, chopped

Soak apricots in wine and set aside in a dish. Rinse chicken pieces under cold water and pat dry. Season the chicken with the dry seasonings and place pieces in a single layer in a large roasting pan. Add onions and carrots. Bake at 350° in a preheated oven for 45 minutes, until the chicken is just beginning to brown. Pour off excess fat and pour apricots and wine over chicken pieces. Baste with juices, finish cooking 30 more minutes, and remove from oven. If not served within 2 hours, chill and bring back to room temperature before reheating.

To reheat, place the chicken in covered pan or oven-proof serving dish with cooking juices (you may skim fat again) and reheat at 375° for 20–30 minutes while first courses are being served. To serve, place the chicken pieces on a serving dish and scrape up pan residue and juice, adding more stock or wine to deglaze if necessary. Pour sauce over chicken and arrange apricots for garnish.
Serves 8.

CARROT TSIMMES

Anne Madorsky adds sweet potatoes, beef bones, orange marmalade, and apricots to her tsimmes and gives the mixture a long baking in her oven—a very traditional approach. The recipe offered here has many of the same savory flavors but produces a lighter side dish to enjoy among the many rich courses in the Seder meal.

8 cups carrots (about 3 pounds),
    peeled and sliced in 1/2 inch
    slices
1 cup orange juice
2 cups prunes
1 cup chicken stock
3 tablespoons honey
1/4 teaspoon nutmeg
2 tablespoons margarine
    (optional)
1/2 teaspoon salt
a generous grating of fresh
    pepper

Bring a large pot filled with water to boil on top of the stove. Drop in sliced carrots and boil for 8 minutes. Drain the carrots in colander and return to the pot, and add remaining ingredients. Simmer together on top of stove for about 30 minutes, or until carrots are tender and flavors are well blended. Check for seasonings and serve, or set aside to be reheated just before serving time.
Serves 10.

CHAROSET

The making of charoset is a highly individualized and tactile process—not unlike making the mortar it symbolizes. The quantities listed below are merely suggestions—don't worry—it's almost impossible to fail at charoset.

3 pounds apples (about 3 cups
    chopped)
2 cups nuts (pecans or walnuts)
3/4 teaspoon cinnamon
1/4 cup Passover wine
1/3 cup honey

Peel and core the apples and chop them in a wooden bowl with a chopper or on a cutting board with a knife. Chop the nuts as well and add

to apples with remaining seasonings. Adjust honey and cinnamon to taste. Cover and store the charoset in a refrigerator until ready to serve. **Makes about 9 cups.**

ANNE MADORSKY'S PASSOVER CHOCOLATE CAKE

The dessert table at the Madorsky Passover is legendary. Beautifully displayed before the service begins, it serves as an incentive to quiet fidgety children and inspire weary adults.

  10 eggs, separated
  1 cup sugar
  6 ounces semisweet chocolate
  2 cups chopped nuts (pecans,
    walnuts or hazelnuts will do)
  1/2 cup chopped toasted nuts for
    garnish

In a mixing bowl, beat the egg yolks and sugar until thick with an electric mixer or whisk. Melt the chocolate in a saucepan over simmering water or in a microwave. Fold the chocolate into the egg mixture, then add the chopped nuts. In a separate bowl, beat the egg whites until stiff but not dry and fold into the chocolate-egg mixture.

Place batter in a greased 10-inch springform pan and bake 1 hour at 350° in a preheated oven. The cake

Anne's Flourless Cheesecake, assorted macaroons, Stewed Fruits, and a nutcake. All the desserts are made without leavening, as is everything eaten during Passover.

is done when it springs back when touched in the center. Cool in its pan on a cake rack.

To serve, remove from pan and place on a serving plate. Garnish with more chopped toasted nuts, melted chocolate or freshly sliced strawberries if desired.
Serves 10–12.

ANNE MADORSKY'S FLOURLESS CHEESECAKE

butter
1/4 cup ground hazelnuts
3–4 packages cream cheese
  (12–16 ounces)
1 1/2 cups sugar
4 large eggs
juice of half a lemon (about 2
  tablespoons)
1/2 teaspoon vanilla

Grease a 2-quart soufflé dish evenly with butter. Place hazelnuts in the dish and shake from side to side to coat the top and sides.

In a mixing bowl, beat the cream cheese until smooth with an electric mixer. Add the sugar slowly, then eggs, then lemon and vanilla flavorings, continuing to beat until batter is smooth. Pour the cake batter into the prepared pan. Place the cake pan in the pan of hot water in a preheated 325° oven for 1 1/4 to 1 1/2 hours.

Shut off the oven and leave the cake in the oven for another 20 minutes. Remove and cool on wire rack. When completely cool, place a serving plate on top and invert. The cake should slip out easily. The cake may be served plain, or you may cover it with sliced fresh strawberries and drizzle 1/2 cup of hot red currant or strained strawberry jam over the top and let it run down the sides.
Makes about 12 servings.

NOTE: *Many recipes are discovered by accident—and we found that using only 3 packages of cream cheese and baking the shorter time produces a lighter version of this wonderful cake.*

PASSOVER STEWED FRUITS

Fruit desserts are often found at the Seder because they are a light aftermath to a traditionally heavy meal, and they can be served without benefit of leavening. Elaine Silverstein calls this popular family recipe "virtually foolproof," and it is. Don't be afraid to experiment with flavorings such as allspice, orange, and a little clove when you try to create your own family recipe.

3 pounds mixed dried fruit such
  as prunes, apricots, pears,
  peaches, and white raisins
1/2 cup sugar
1 lemon, thinly sliced
1 cinnamon stick
water to cover

SOUR CREAM SAUCE
2 cups sour cream

4 tablespoons brown sugar
1/2 teaspoon vanilla
1 tablespoon Cointreau
  (optional)

Place fruits in a large pot. Add the sugar, lemon slices, and cinnamon. Add just enough water to cover the mixture. Simmer over low heat until soft—about 1 hour. Meanwhile, mix ingredients for the sour cream sauce and chill. Remove fruits to a serving bowl and chill until ready to serve with optional sour cream sauce.
Serves 10–12.

Greens, a symbolic part of every Seder meal, are represented by asparagus this year.

The wonders of Easter are sweetest on a little child's face.

*L*ike certain songs we love because hearing them brings back important moments from our past, certain holidays resonate with deeply personal memories. Easter acquired such a significance for George Butler and Sally Flocks early in their married life.

"We woke up on our first Easter morning in Atlanta and on our front steps was an Easter basket. Not a big basket, but beautifully decorated," George remembers. "There was no note. Yet year in and year out a lovely basket appeared at our door." Although they tried to figure out whom the basket was from, they have never discovered their benefactor's identity. "Easter's always had special magical connotations because of those baskets. So seldom in life do we get gifts unannounced," Sally says. "Our yearly Easter Egg Hunt is our payback, our gift to the neighborhood."

As George and Sally tell their story, "Here Comes Peter Cottontail" wafts through an open window and across the back porch of their cottage home. It is mid-morning on Easter Saturday, and they have only a few hours to transform their low-lying backyard into a Beatrix Potter wonderland before leading their friends' and neighbors' children in their tenth annual Easter Egg hunt.

Thanks to a hard rain the night before, the grass is wet and shiny and a little long, just the way the Easter Bunny prefers. While George strings balloons from a porch post to a tree sixty feet away, Sally checks cartons of colored eggs for cracked shells. "I have to start hiding the eggs by 11:00," she says, "in order to be ready by the time the kids come at 2:00."

Three hours may sound like a lot of time to strew eggs across a lawn, but Sally is about to hide a lot of eggs—two hundred plastic ones filled with candy and trinkets, countless bags of foil-wrapped chocolate eggs, and more than thirty dozen real eggs she has boiled and dyed herself. "I've been up to my elbows in eggs all week!" she says. Although Sally has also done a tremendous amount of baking and

"I start hiding the eggs by 11:00 A.M.," Sally explains. "George helps sometimes, but he's usually busy blowing up balloons."

Sally dyes her eggs in four big pots, a dozen eggs per pot at a time. "I'm very particular about the shades."

"I love to bake cakes, but I don't like to have cakes around the house," Sally says, laughing. "It's too dangerous. Dieting is a losing battle."

decorating to prepare for the hunt, "the egg boiling is the hardest work, especially since my stove has only two burners."

Once the eggs are boiled, Sally dyes them in four big pasta pots, a dozen eggs in a pot at a time. "I'm very particular about the colors," she admits with a dimpled smile. In fact, part of the annual preparation includes lighthearted banter between Sally and her mother-in-law, Josephine Butler, over proper shades and dipping times. "Sally wants a certain number red, a certain number green," Mrs. Butler explains, "while I start helter skelter."

Egg dying is only one of the rituals tied to the hunt. Sally and George prepare everything the same way each year. Invitations, for example, always have a picture of black and white sheep with hand-colored pastel eggs. With the last name Flocks, Sally has long had a special affinity for sheep. "I found this card before George and I were married and sent it to him while we were living in different cities." A hint of nostalgia creeps into Sally's voice. Inside the message teases, "If you can find me I'm yours," the perfect sentiment for romance and egg hunting alike.

Like the invitation, the menu does not vary. Sally bakes chocolate, poppyseed, and carrot cakes in the same lamb molds every year. She makes the same cookies—"lots and lots of cookies." With the eggs whose shells have cracked she creates her traditional egg salad bunny head, complete with caviar eyes and whiskers. Mrs. Butler brings her

George is in charge of blowing up balloons and hanging them across the yard; it's a big job, and he takes all the help he can get.

signature cheese biscuits. And there are large pitchers of pink lemonade. In fact, the one new variation this year is the elimination of a spiked punch. George explains, "We used to have some for the adults, but less and less was drunk so we've decided we only need the lemonade."

A debonair lawyer given to bow ties, George has just ribboned off the small area where the toddlers will do their hunting. Now he calls over to Sally. For a few moments they stand together admiring the brightly colored, dimestore balloons gaily waving overhead.

They are a couple used to working and playing side by side. George runs his law practice out of an office in their house, and Sally does free-lance editorial work at home. They also co-edit a legal history journal, even ride a tandem bicycle. Although the switch from individual bikes was originally a practical matter, it has become a source of shared pleasure. "I had a wreck on my own bike because I had an epileptic seizure," explains Sally, disarmingly straightforward about all aspects of her life. "Now we ride together around town and we take the bike on vacations to the mountains. It's a lot of fun."

Not that they are unrealistic about how much togetherness a marriage can take. "We argue," laughs Sally. But not all that often. "The secret to our success at working together," George says, carrying a glass jar full of jelly beans outside, "is that we have distinctly separate roles. We perform our separate tasks and don't look over each other's

The Easter Egg

Have you ever watched an egg hatch? Its seamless shell, impenetrable and lifeless, suddenly cracks open to reveal fragile new life within. What a wonderful symbol, rich with metaphorical connotations! No wonder civilizations throughout history have incorporated the egg into their most joyful celebrations. The ancient religions of India and Egypt held that the world itself began as a huge egg, that when the egg split, the upper half became the heavens and the lower half became earth. Persians, Greeks, and Chinese exchanged eggs, often dyed a brilliant scarlet, at their spring festivals as a sign of return to life after the winter hiatus. Early Christians tied the heart of their faith—belief in Christ's resurrection—to the egg as a symbol that what appears dead contains new life. Considered holy, eggs were blessed and used in the Easter ceremonies, and they were often elaborately decorated. In 1290 the household records for King Edward I of England detail the cost of purchasing 450 eggs to be colored and covered in gold leaf. In Eastern Europe, Easter egg painting has evolved over centuries into a highly developed craft. Eggs are often painted red or white with red patterns, representing Christ's blood and the color of life. European tradition connected the Easter egg with another ancient symbol of spring renewal, the hare. Sacred to the European spring-goddess Eostre, from which Easter takes its name, the hare laid eggs as symbols of fertility and spring renewal on Easter morning. And for hundreds of years, children have been sent out to find those eggs.

shoulder. I take care of the yard before the egg hunt and Sally does the food. Then we come together. The trick is not to poach, to respect the other's assignment."

That the Easter Egg Hunt, their major entertaining effort of the year, centers on children—although they are childless themselves—tells a great deal about George and Sally as people. "It may make it more meaningful to us because we don't have kids," muses Sally. "It's a real opportunity to do things with children, and we really love spending time with them."

George considers the magnetic hold the annual event has over the children, as well as accompanying adults, who attend year after year. "Children are very perceptive," he says, "and they pick up on the fact that these adults—us—don't have any ostensible reason for doing this." He and Sally head back to their assigned tasks, Sally hiding eggs, George hammering signs into the damp earth to warn children away from danger spots.

⁓

Shortly before 2:00, the first guests begin to spiral down a set of stone steps, marked by a carrot-festooned sign directing them from the sidewalk to the "Hole Sweet Hole."

There is no getting around it, Sally and George's backyard is, well,

Fifteen minutes before the first guests arrive, Sally disappears into the house to take on her new persona, "the Easter Bunny."

in a hole. "When we bought this lot about ten years ago, everyone kidded us about buying a hole. We just thought it would be a great place for an Easter egg hunt," Sally explains with a toss of her ears.

Yes, ears. The scholarly editor with a Ph.D. in history sports whiskers and long floppy ears, her traditional egg hunt attire. Transformed into "the Easter Bunny," she waits by a small table at the foot of the steps to greet little girls in flowered dresses and little boys firmly gripping their straw baskets. Each child guesses how many jelly beans are in the big glass jar on the table before putting on a name tag.

"We have the name tags because I

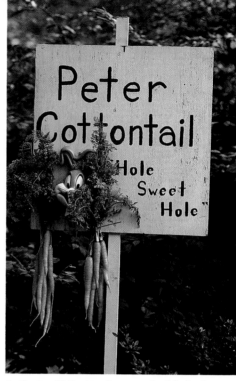

A giant rabbit sign festooned with fresh carrots points egg hunters down a winding stone path into George and Sally's garden.

After the toddlers and three- and four-year-olds are given an early start, the older kids are turned loose to hunt.

like being able to talk to the kids by their first name and find out what they've been up to," George says. "It's also fun to see the parents in the children, how they behave, how rambunctious they are, how polite. By and large they're little miniatures of their parents." He and Sally chronicle the years of egg hunts in shoeboxes full of photographs. "We keep pictures so we can see the kids from year to year and chart their progression."

Sally and George did not set out to create a tradition. "The first year we held a hunt we were in our late twenties, and we really did think it would be for people our age. Then people we knew started having kids. By the second year it was more for the kids, although the adults, especially the adults without kids, would go look for eggs after the kids left. Now I have single friends who borrow kids to come. They get a lot of joy out of it."

By the fourth year Sally knew she and George had created something larger than themselves. "It was the year before we moved into this house," Sally remembers, "when it was still under construction. Plus, I was teaching high school for the first time and didn't feel I had time. We told ourselves we had to skip the hunt."

George picks up the story. "We didn't send out invitations. Then about ten days before Easter, some of our friends sheepishly asked what our plans were because they wanted to go out of town but their children insisted on remaining here for the Easter egg hunt."

"We recognized it was something that couldn't die out," Sally says, "once we heard from the parents how upsetting it was for the kids when we didn't have it."

As more and more children arrive, George and Sally make sure they stay behind a roped-off area away from the eggs. Of course, there are plenty of cookies and jelly beans to keep everyone occupied. The scene has an old-fashioned, innocent charm as the children in party clothes try to stay on best behavior, sipping lemonade while stealing glances across the lawn to scan for pastel clues.

When the level of tingling anticipation is just at the verge of becoming more than the children, or par-

ents, can bear, George blows his wooden train whistle and announces, "Train's about to leave the station." A few grownups look around confused, but the kids know exactly what's up. First the toddlers are let into their private section. Then the three- and four-year-olds are given a head start. Finally, as the recorded music crescendos into "The Bunny Hop," George opens the floodgates and children pour across the lawn.

The parents hang back at the sidelines, among them Bill Haley, who's been coming to hunts since before he had children of his own. "Our son John was a little mad at us today because we were running late. One year we came after the egg hunt. He was afraid that was going to happen again."

Prepared for such emergencies, Sally always has several dozen extra eggs hidden away in the

Enough eggs are hidden for each child to find half a dozen. Easter Bunny Sally helps children whose baskets are a little on the empty side as the hunt winds down.

kitchen to bring out just in case there are a few latecomers. And to make sure no one heads home empty basketed, "The Easter Bunny" wanders among the children as the hunt winds down, offering welcome clues to anyone whose basket is not yet overflowing. No child goes home with less than half a dozen eggs.

The search lasts longer than most adults would expect. Even when many of the children have been lured away by the promise of cookies and games, lemonade and slices of cake, a handful of boys and girls continues to search for that last elusive egg. Nevertheless, Sally makes a prediction. "For weeks afterwards, we always find eggs that were missed. I'm sure there are lots still out there."

In an informal ceremony, she hands out a chocolate rabbit to the child who finds the "golden egg," a special egg Sally has blown hollow and specially painted before hiding. Another rabbit goes to the child who comes closest to guessing the number of jelly beans in the jar. Then it is time for George to coordinate the games.

Though the kids do not all know each other, they join right in the egg-on-the-spoon races, drawn by George's energy and enthusiasm. "We have hula hoops set up, too," George tells them as soon as the race is over. "The point is to see how many times you can get your frisbee through the hoops." Not many, unless you're short, freckled, and under ten, but winning is not the point. Their baskets care-

Even when many of the children have been lured away by cookies and games, a handful continues to search for that last elusive egg.

fully tucked away, the kids nibble cookies and cake, balance eggs on their spoons, pop jelly beans in their mouths by the handful, and generally delight in the perfect spring day.

If pure joy is a central element of genuine celebration, children are much better at expressing it than most adults. As George says, gazing across his lawn peppered with small, bright-cheeked egg balancers, "You can always trust kids' instincts. Either they enjoy themselves or they don't." These kids are having a ball.

Adam Hansen competes intensely in the egg race.

According to Mike Schroeder, who's been coming to the hunt as long he can remember, "George is totally exuberant. He gets right down on the kids' level. The kids don't all know each other, but when George organizes all these wild games for them to participate in, they love it."

An Easter Egg "Tea Party"

Josephine Butler's Cheese Biscuits

Egg Salad "Bunny" with Caviar and Crackers

Chocolate Lamb Cake

Poppy Seed Lamb Cake

Carrot Cupcakes

Sally's Sugar Cookies

Brown Bunny Cookies

Easter Eggs

Pink Lemonade for a Crowd

JOSEPHINE BUTLER'S CHEESE BISCUITS

The grownups at Sally and George's especially look forward to the cheese biscuits that George's mother, Josephine Butler, makes each year. The pecans make a particularly savory addition to the centers of these rich golden cookies.

1 pound aged Cheddar cheese
3/4 pound margarine (3 sticks)
4–5 cups all-purpose flour, sifted
1/8 to 1/2 teaspoon cayenne pepper
pecan halves or pieces

Grate the cheddar cheese on the large holes of a hand grater. Place in a bowl and cream together with the margarine. Add the flour and pepper, using enough flour so the dough is not too sticky to handle but holds together well.

Break off walnut-sized pieces, roll between your palms into a ball, and flatten on a cookie sheet that is lined with baking parchment. You may also use a cookie press to form the cookies directly on the pan.

Bake cookies in a preheated 350° oven for 20 minutes until edges and bottoms are lightly browned. Press pecan halves into the center of each cookie while still hot and remove to a rack to cool.
Makes about 4 dozen cookies.

EGG SALAD "BUNNY" WITH CAVIAR AND CRACKERS

Sally enjoys making all of her Easter food into whimsical animal shapes—especially rabbits. This recipe works just as well in a more conventional circle for other occasions, using the caviars in your own garnish design on top. Here, sour cream is substituted for the mayonnaise in Sally's recipe to decrease the likelihood that the salad will spoil in an outdoor setting.

1 dozen hard-boiled eggs
1 1/2 cups sour cream (you may use a "light" version)
salt and pepper to taste
2 ounces black caviar
2 ounces red caviar
crackers
chopped green onions or chives for garnish

Peel the cooled hard-boiled eggs and chop them in a food processor or by hand with a knife into uniformly medium-sized pieces (pea-sized is okay). Fold in the sour cream and season to taste with salt and freshly ground pepper.

Trace the outline of a rabbit face with ears on a piece of baking parchment or waxed paper. Cut out the outline and place on a large platter or flat wooden board. Spread the egg mixture over the pattern, gouging out indentations for rabbit eyes, nose, ears, and mouth. Drain each of the caviars on separate paper towels to reduce the running of the dyes in the caviar. Fill the mouth

Any eggs that crack during the boiling/dyeing process go into the egg salad bunny head. "The parents seem particularly partial to the egg salad. For the nose and eyes I use black caviar, for the ears and mouth red caviar."

and ear cavities with the red caviar and fill the nose and eyes with the black caviar.

Garnish the plate with chopped green onions or chives. Cover with plastic wrap and chill until ready to serve. Spread on your choice of table crackers. If you like, you can serve a little leftover caviar on the side.

NOTE: Do not leave eggs unrefrigerated for long periods of time or in a sunny spot. It's best to bring this dish to the table after your guests have all arrived.
Serves 15–20 adults.

SALLY'S SUGAR COOKIES

Sally uses this dough for all the whimsical Easter shapes she serves on her table—bunnies, chicks, eggs, and lambs. Each is then hand-decorated with ready-made tubes of colored frostings to accent the delightful animal faces. It is a time-consuming process, but one that is always appreciated by her young guests.

"We make lots and lots of cookies. Decorating them is such fun, kind of like fingerpainting," Sally says. The plain and chocolate cookies show up as tulips, sheep, bunnies, and hatching chicks.

1/4 pound unsalted butter, cut in
  6 or 8 pieces
1 cup sugar
1 egg
1 tablespoon milk
1/2 teaspoon vanilla extract
1/8 teaspoon salt
1/2 teaspoon baking powder
2 1/4–2 3/4 cups all-purpose flour

Place butter and sugar in a mixing bowl or the bowl of a food processor. Beat with mixer or process until combined. Add the egg, milk, and vanilla and blend. Mix together dry ingredients (using the smaller amount of flour) and gradually add to the bowl, mixing or processing after each addition. Check for consistency of dough. If too soft and sticky for rolling, add more flour. If your kitchen is especially warm, you may want to refrigerate the dough for an hour before handling.

Place dough on floured surface and roll out with floured rolling pin to 1/8 inch thickness. Cut into desired shapes and place on baking parchment paper on a cookie sheet. Bake in a preheated 375° oven for about 8 minutes. Cool on a wire rack and decorate with frosting. ***Makes 16–20 cookies, depending on size of cutters.***

BROWN BUNNY COOKIES

To make the chocolate version of Sally's Sugar Cookies, add 1/3 cup of unsweetened cocoa before adding the flour to the above recipe. Bake in a preheated 325° oven for about 8 minutes.

EASTER EGGS

One of Sally's biggest jobs is boiling and dyeing hundreds of eggs. She recommends allowing at least 6 eggs per child. Dyeing can be as elaborate as you wish, but for this number, an assortment of six or eight colors is plenty, as you may vary the results with how long the eggs are immersed.

eggs at room temperature
red, blue, and yellow food
  coloring
vinegar
hot water

BOILING THE EGGS
To reduce the possibility of broken shells, prick the bottom (larger end) of each egg before cooking. This can be done with a gadget designed for this purpose or with a clean hat pin or needle and thimble. Carefully place several dozen eggs in a large pot and fill with cold water to cover. Place the pot on a stove burner over medium-high heat. When the water comes to a boil, reduce heat and simmer for 15 minutes. Remove eggs from heat and place immediately in another pot or sink filled with ice water to chill thoroughly. Remove any cracked or broken eggs (they can be used for your egg salad), and place eggs back in car-

tons in refrigerator until ready to dye. Repeat process until all the eggs are cooked and cooled.

COLORING THE EGGS

For each color bath you choose, use about 1/2 ounce of food coloring (1/2 of a 1-ounce bottle) to about 8 cups of hot water and 1/4 cup vinegar. Dip eggs in until desired shade is reached, return the eggs to their cartons for storage, and continue until all the eggs are colored. The colors should not run once they are dried. Below are some color formulas popular at Easter time to add to your single shades of yellow, pink, blue, and green:

    violet - 1 part red, 2 parts blue
    purple - 3 parts red, 1 part blue
    turquoise - 1 part green, 3 parts
      blue
    orange - 2 parts yellow, 1 part red

PINK LEMONADE FOR A CROWD

    2 cups water
    4 cups sugar
    3 1/2 cups lemon juice*
    1/2 to 1 tablespoon frozen grape
      juice concentrate
    4 lemons, sliced

If you are not up to squeezing 15–20 lemons for their juice, an acceptable substitute is the frozen bottled juice found in your grocery.

Place the water and sugar in a pot and boil together for 2 minutes on top

It wouldn't be an Easter egg hunt without sparkling pitchers of lemonade.

of the stove. Chill the syrup or let it come to room temperature. Pour the syrup into a large stock pot or beverage container and add the lemon juice and 2 gallons of cold water. Stir in grape juice concentrate and watch the color change to a delightful shade of pink. You may experiment to get just the right color by starting with

the smaller amount. Store in refrigerator, or, if there isn't room, cover the container and keep in a cool location for up to 8 hours before using. Add some ice and lemon slices to a glass pitcher and pour in the lemonade when ready to serve.
Makes about 30–40 8-ounce servings.

"She's the central figure," says Bill Jameison of his mother, Phyllis Bostick.

*O*ther people's families. So often they seem happier, less complicated than our own. As kids we wondered why our parents were not more like Dorothy's down the block. We wondered why we were stuck with our brothers and sisters instead of lucking out with Jeff's across the street. Sitting down to a meal, whether school-night meat loaf or Thanksgiving turkey, we wondered why our family didn't share the natural comraderie of the families we watched on television. Now, with our parents aging and our brothers and sisters scattered, we wonder, even as we struggle to raise a family of our own, if disintegration of that frail bond is inevitable.

Phyllis Bostick's four children grew up with no happier, perhaps even less happy, memories of their family than most of us. Then, late in life, after two marriages and much self-examination, Phyllis Bostick set out to create new memories. Over the last eleven years she has succeeded by rekindling and refining a basic maternal function—feeding her children a good meal. But what a meal.

On a late Friday afternoon in San Francisco, the setting sun streams through the bay windows of Phyllis's small third-floor walk-up apartment. In the dining alcove, off limits until tomorrow night's formal meal, the table is already set with fine china and silver cutlery. Her children are assembled in the living room: Bill Jameison, the baby of the family, who's driven up from Los Angeles; Linda Jameison, an urbane Manhattan attorney; Susan Jameison, the oldest, who, following the rules that allow each child one adult companion, has brought husband Frank; and Kathy Blankenship and husband Steve, who arrive breathless from fighting a traffic jam to make it on time from nearby Davis.

Phyllis hands out old pictures and report cards from a box of mementos she recently uncovered. No one under thirty-nine years old is present, yet in the nervous energy building beneath the siblings' casual conversation pulses the anticipation of children waiting for the grown-up to take charge and make the excitement happen.

Promptly at 5:30, Phyllis brings out the champagne, glasses are raised in a toast, and "The Dinner" weekend has begun. The air is full of happy expectation over the whirlwind schedule of togetherness ahead.

It wasn't always so in the Bostick family.

"Celebration was left out when the kids were growing up," Phyllis acknowledges, sadly. "We had a few traditions but it was difficult to do things as a family. We did not have an outgoing, warm family."

"There had never been any encouragement of togetherness," Linda remembers, "and off and on,

"When I was a kid, coming home from school I never had any idea what we'd have for dinner," says Bill, holding up an old photograph of himself from a box of mementos Phyllis recently uncovered.

According to Kathy, "The food makes it special, but what makes it special, too, is knowing how much Mom enjoys doing this."

"The dinner has cemented things," according to oldest daughter Susan. "We feel like a family for the first time in ways I never felt growing up."

"If it ever became a task, I'd quit right then," Phyllis says, relishing the effort she puts into each detail of the meal.

one of us would not talk to another for periods of time. But after Frank [Phyllis's second husband] died, none of that stuff seemed important. We rallied around mother."

Meanwhile Phyllis set her own agenda. "I began to think of ways to get the family together so we could be happy more instead of having all these terrible memories." The first formal dinner she made for just her children and herself was in 1979, a lavish feast to celebrate and thank Bill for remodeling her kitchen. The gathering was a big success. "I thought maybe we should do it again the next year, so we did. It became obvious we were going to do it every year. Then it kind of grew."

What everyone continues to refer to as "The Dinner" has developed into a three-day celebration—an extended weekend for Phyllis and her grown children to be together without outside distractions, eating and playing and talking. The particulars of the weekend's structure have evolved organically over time. "None of the weekend's traditions have any significant foundations," jokes Bill. Yet the resulting strict if subtle and often lighthearted rituals carefully orchestrated by Phyllis bring the family closer together without any questions. In fact, they're followed with childlike glee.

"The whole thing is a ritual," explains Susan, ticking off the schedule of meals and procedures she has come to expect. "We meet Friday evening. We breeze in on Saturday in time for lunch. That's succeeded by time to ourselves. Then we reconvene for cocktails with other guests as an extra element of surprise. Then there's the dinner. And the picnic Sunday. And more often than not, we're also celebrating a birthday."

This year Bill, the baby of the family, hits the big four-oh. According to family custom, Bill, like his sisters before him, must receive forty presents for forty years, so the process of gift opening on Friday evening is a slow one. Bill savors each present between sips of champagne and everyone inspects the various gifts: collectibles, copies of *Popular Mechanics* and baseball cards from the year he was born, fancy wines, vinegars, and foodstuffs. But the biggest hit is the forty-first gift, which Phyllis says Bill deserves according to Chinese tradition—a giant box filled with jars of her homemade pickles.

Despite all the laughter when Linda brings out the store-bought cake mistakenly inscribed "In Simpathy [*sic*]," the family is still getting used to being together again. Sisters and brother are on best behavior, affectionate but a little shy. It takes time to get in sync with each other's rhythms. "Because there were not strong bonds among us when we were young, the bonds started after we left home," Susan says. "We didn't really know each other before." Each year the weekend process of the dinner brings them closer.

By late Saturday morning—the wine tasting and early lunch of cold

Coming back to their mother's apartment loaded down with bags of picnic fixings, Linda, Susie, Billy, Kathy, Frank, and Steve clown around like teenagers.

salads—everyone is already more used to one another, at ease and genuinely enjoying being together. When at precisely 1:00 P.M. Phyllis closes herself in the kitchen, the rest of the family dawdles by the front door, not quite ready to go their separate ways. But they know the rules. Saturday afternoon Phyllis has the apartment to herself to put the finishing touches on that night's big meal, the original excuse for the weekend gathering and still its anchor event.

She begins planning one dinner as soon as, if not before, the last is over. She never makes the same dish

Phyllis begins planning one dinner as soon as, if not before, last year's is over.

The Family Dinner

WHILE LARGE HOLIDAY CELEBRATIONS—CHRISTMAS, THANKSGIVING, THE FOURTH OF JULY—CREATE THEIR OWN MEMORIES, WHAT BRINGS AND HOLDS MOST FAMILIES TOGETHER ARE THE SMALL RITUALS SHARED IN DAILY LIFE. THE KILLER GAME OF MONOPOLY, THE HALF HOUR SET ASIDE TO READ ALOUD, THE SINGING IN THE CAR ON LONG TRIPS. FAMILY RITUALS CAN BE AS SIMPLE AS WATCHING THE SUNSET OR WASHING THE DOG, AS LONG AS EVERYONE CAN COUNT ON THAT TIME WHEN THE FAMILY COMES FIRST AND THERE ARE NO DISTRACTIONS. PERHAPS THE EPITOME OF WHAT HAS BECOME KNOWN AS "QUALITY TIME" IS THE FAMILY DINNER, A MEAL OF HEARTY EATING, WHETHER A HOME-COOKED ROAST, TAKE-OUT PIZZA, OR SATURDAY MORNING BREAKFAST AT A LOCAL DINER, THAT CREATES LIVELY CONVERSATION AND GENUINE INTIMACY. ∽ IF YOURS IS ONE OF THE MANY FAMILIES, LIKE OUR OWN, WHO FIND IT DIFFICULT TO GET EVERYBODY TO SIT DOWN AT THE SAME MEAL TOGETHER, YOU MIGHT WANT TO FOLLOW THE EXAMPLE OF A FLEXIBLE WOMAN WE KNOW WHO HAS EVOLVED A TRADITION OF TAKING TEA WITH HER SCHOOL-AGE DAUGHTERS. THEIR RITUAL IS COZY AND ELEGANT WITH SPECIAL TEA CUPS AND SERVING PIECES. THE ONE VARIABLE IS WHEN TEA-TIME OCCURS. MORNING, AFTERNOON, AND THE MIDDLE OF THE NIGHT ARE ALL EQUALLY ACCEPTABLE AS LONG AS THE FAMILY IS ALL AT HOME TOGETHER.

When Linda appears in her mother's formal gown, Phyllis, Kathy and Susan gather around her, touching the fabric, adjusting the bow, giggling together as if they were about to send Linda off to her first dance.

"One of the reasons we come and enjoy it so much," says Linda, "is that we love our mother. It took some years of growing up to realize she's the stable force."

twice and takes no requests because, as she says, "They're not supposed to know what's happening."

"I was up visiting months ago," recalls Bill. "I saw two large stacks, there had to be twenty, cookbooks on the kitchen table and she said to me, 'Somewhere in there is your dinner.'"

Virtually the only job Phyllis will delegate is to allow Linda to write out the menu on small ceramic stands. Linda bought them for her mother a few years ago, and they have become a traditional part of the table setting. At seventy-one, Phyllis still scours the city for exactly the right ingredients, then prepares all eleven courses from scratch by herself in her tiny kitchen. She takes three days just to set the table. Skilled at handicrafts, she creates a new centerpiece for each dinner and carefully selects individual grown-up "party favors" that she places at each place.

"The dinner is kind of a gift from me to the kids, but it's more than money can buy. If it was just a gift of food, I could take the money and buy them something," Phyllis explains. "This is putting part of me in, a gift of time, and talent."

The eleven-course dinner on Saturday evening is the climax of the weekend, "more a happening or experience than a meal," as Kathy describes it. Everyone dresses up a little. Linda emerges from her mother's bedroom in a gown Phyllis once wore to the opera.

At seven sharp everyone finally gets to see the table. Candles are lit, the table settings and fresh lime pyramid centerpiece are admired, the personal gifts are taken from pretty flowered bags and shown around. As another toast is raised

Linda's annual assignment is to write out the elaborate menu on ceramic stands.

Only Phyllis is allowed to serve on Saturday night. The meal is her gift to give and hers to orchestrate.

and the meal begins, Phyllis sits at the head of the table smiling in the candlelight.

Soon she is everywhere: serving, cooking, clearing, loading the dishwasher. "You know you're not supposed to do that," she says laughing, scolding Linda four courses later when she places a dish in front of Kathy. Everyone is expected to help clear one course, one at a time in revolving order around the table. But only Phyllis

is allowed to serve. The meal is her gift to give and hers to orchestrate. The teasing secrecy with which she offers each exotically named dish keeps the dinner playful and spiced with mystery.

"She's the central figure, and not just by cooking," Bill says as Phyllis carries in a platter. "She's the one making the effort to get us together." He pauses with a tinge of filial wickedness in his voice. "Also she gets to show off a little."

The pace she sets is leisurely. The mood is boisterous, with large dollops of the laughter and joking that they remember were forbidden at their childhood table. Phyllis sets only one rule, to try three bites of every dish. She has learned to keep portions small, both of food and wine. A new wine is served with each course, often from a winery run by friends.

This year's meal begins with jambon persille. Then come sweet

As Bill fries up sausages, no one cares that outdoor plans have been rained out. The "kids" set up their earthy picnic at the same table where they ate so elegantly the night before.

onion soup, crab cakes with tomato sherry sauce, and penne with porcini, Pecorino cheese, and pancetta. The fifth course is sweet-and-sour casserole of buffalo tongue—Phyllis always tries to include an exotic surprise—which leads to roasted lamb with balsamic-glazed onions and mustard kale. By now the table needs a break, so Phyllis offers sangrita sorbet. She is unhappy with the Celery Victor that follows, but unanimous praise erupts for the sautéed goat cheese with pink peppercorns and port wine sauce.

Late in the meal, when it is hard to believe anyone has room for chocolate soufflé and hazelnut crepes, one of the sisters jokes, "This is an endurance test." Not exactly, but the siblings do exude a sense of bonding, as if they've made it together through a strenuous group experience.

The final course is always a savory tidbit served after the sweet dessert. At 11:30, as the Angels On Horseback, oysters wrapped in bacon, are cleared, the children clap and cheer for their mother. Gazing out across the table of faces, Phyllis beams back in satisfaction and love.

Sunday is no anticlimax. At 10:30 A.M. on the dot—punctuality is crucial to the weekend's structure—everyone gathers again. On the coffee table sits a magnificent "black cake," a version of fruit cake Phyllis began preparing months ahead, and still another pile of gifts, this time for Kathy's birthday. Because Phyllis purposely schedules her dinner in June when Bill and Kathy's birthdays fall, the weekend supplies a variety of family celebration rituals.

A few minutes before 11:00, Phyllis gets out a roll of crisp bills and hands them out like weekly allowances. While she takes sole responsibility for the dinner, the kids work together to put together the Sunday picnic. Hair loose and unkempt, faces scrubbed without makeup, in jeans and sneakers, they pile in the car to head to Macy's Cellar. Naturally they get lost on the way, like teenagers. Not one of them seems over seventeen years old. Bill has become Billy again, Susan, Susie. In the store they plot who will buy what in order to feast within their mother's established budget.

Bad weather has forced the picnic indoors, but no one cares. It is enough to be together. Bill fries up some sausage while the others set

What her children may enjoy most this weekend is seeing Phyllis's pleasure in bringing them together.

out the salmon and olives and crusty bread. Classical music plays on the radio. Conversation and laughter flow, everyone relaxed and easy.

For Phyllis Bostick, sharing this moment is what the weekend is all about. "All those years I wished we had closeness and good times. I guess I'm trying to catch up having the kids together. I think they feel the same way."

Kathy makes it clear they do. "The food makes it very special, but what makes it special, too, is knowing how much Mom enjoys doing this. She gets such pleasure out of it that it gives us a lot of pleasure. And that's really, really neat."

Phyllis Bostick's Family Dinner

Cilantro-Spiked Tapenade

Belle Rhodes' Caviar Roulade

Crab and Scallop Cakes with

Wasabe Cream

Fresh Pea Soup with Mint

Roasted Leg of Lamb with Rosemary

Balsamic Onions

Sautéed Kale

Sweet Potato and Rice Vinegar Salad

Angels on Horseback

Raspberry-Filled Meringue Hearts

Phyllis Bostick has been preparing these elaborate dinners since 1979, and each year's menu has contained nine to eleven different dishes. Researching most of her recipes from cookbooks and food magazines, Phyllis Bostick has prepared and her family has sampled more than a hundred dishes. The menu below represents dishes drawn from this year's celebration, samples from previous years' favorites, and those designed to "round out" the menu for inclusion in this book.

CILANTRO-SPIKED TAPENADE

This dip was invented by accident when Phyllis Bostick's daughter Kathy used cilantro instead of parsley in her recipe. The results were well received and the dip is now expected at their annual gatherings. The sauce also makes a wonderful topping for hot or cold pasta and chicken.

1/2 cup cilantro leaves, (or one
  large handful)
2 garlic cloves
3/4 cup coarsely chopped onion
1 can of tuna (6 1/2 ounce size),
  drained
1/2 cup pitted black olives
1/4 cup capers
1 cup mayonnaise
2 teaspoons anchovy paste
freshly ground black pepper
1/4 cup lemon juice
grated zest of 2 lemons

In a food processor, combine the cilantro and garlic and pulse together until finely chopped. Add the onion, tuna, olives, and capers and pulse several times to chop and blend; do not purée. Transfer ingredients to a bowl and beat in mayonnaise, anchovy paste, pepper, lemon juice, and zest. Chill several hours to blend flavors before serving as a dip with vegetables or crackers. **Makes approximately 2 1/2 cups.**

CRAB & SCALLOP CAKES WITH WASABE CREAM

Phyllis Bostick's "secret" for achieving the rich texture of her crab cakes is to use puréed scallops to bind the ingredients. The wasabe (green horseradish sauce) is a popular ingredient in the local East-West cuisines of California.

2 tablespoons chopped parsley
1/2 cup chopped scallions
1/2 pound scallops
1/4 teaspoon cayenne pepper
juice of 1 lemon
1 pound lump crab meat
1/2 cup coarse, dried bread
  crumbs
2–3 tablespoons butter
1–2 tablespoons vegetable oil

WASABE CREAM
2 tablespoons mixed green onion
  and parsley, minced
3 tablespoons oil
2–3 teaspoons wasabe paste,
  mixed according to directions*
4 tablespoons lemon juice

1 cup sour cream
scallions for garnish

*You may substitute 4 tablespoons of premixed wasabe that comes in a tube. The key is to add the right amount for your taste, so experiment by adding a small amount at a time.

Mince parsley and scallions in a food processor and transfer to another mixing bowl. Purée scallops in processor, adding cayenne pepper and lemon juice to blend. Mix the scallop mixture in with the parsley and scallions and blend in the crab meat by hand. Mold mixture into cakes using about 1/4 cup at a time. Coat the cakes with bread crumbs that have been placed in a flat bowl, and store prepared crab cakes, covered and on waxed paper, in the refrigerator until ready to cook.

To make the sauce, process parsley and green onions, oil, and wasabe in food processor until smooth. Add the lemon juice and sour cream and blend. Set aside.

At serving time, melt the butter and oil in a frying pan and heat until sizzling. Add a layer of crab cakes and sauté until golden on each side—about 2 minutes each side. Drain the crab cakes on paper towels and keep in a warm oven (about 200°) until all the crab cakes are done. To serve, spoon a small amount of the sauce in the bottom of each serving dish, top with crab cakes and garnish with scallions. **Serves 5–6 as main course or 10 to 12 as appetizers.**

BELLE RHODES' CAVIAR ROULADE

Belle Rhodes, whose cooking skill inspired Phyllis when she first began serious "gourmet" cooking, taught this recipe to Phyllis. The recipe was originally adapted from Craig Claiborne's New York Times Menu Cookbook (Harper and Row). It is an elegant appetizer for special dinner celebrations and was a favorite among the many dishes Phyllis has prepared for her annual dinners.

4 tablespoons butter
1/2 cup flour
2 cups milk
4 large eggs, separated
4 ounces cream cheese
1 cup sour cream
4 ounces good-quality caviar
1/4 cup finely minced green onion

Preheat oven to 325°, placing a rack near the bottom of the oven. Grease a 10 x 15 baking sheet or line the pan with greased and floured waxed paper or a sheet of baking parchment.

In a saucepan, melt butter over medium heat. Blend in the flour with a wire whisk, then add the milk and cook, stirring constantly until the mixture boils. Reduce heat to low and simmer one minute longer. Remove from heat. Beat the egg yolks slightly, add to the milk mixture, and cool.

Beat the egg whites with an electric mixer or wire whisk until stiff and fold carefully into the cooled milk mixture. Spread the batter in the prepared pan and bake on a lower oven rack about 20–30 minutes.

When the cake is lightly browned and springs back when touched with your finger, turn out onto a sheet of waxed paper. Meanwhile, prepare the filling. Mix the cream cheese with about 3 tablespoons of the sour cream. Add half of the caviar. When the cake has cooled slightly, spread the cake with the filling mixture and roll up jelly roll fashion. Serve the roulade in slices, adding a dollop of sour cream, additional caviar, and a sprinkling of green onion.

NOTE: Be sure to wipe your slicing knife after each slice to keep the filling from smearing on each slice.
Serves 10–12.

FRESH PEA SOUP WITH MINT

Since the Bostick dinner often takes place in spring or early summer, fresh peas are readily available. Family members recall pea soup as a favorite from some years ago.

3 cups chicken or ham stock
3/4 pound fresh, shelled peas
  (about 3 pounds unshelled)
1/2 cup peeled and minced
  carrots
1/2 cup minced onion
1 cup peeled and minced parsnips
1/2 cup cream
1 tablespoon chopped fresh mint
1/4 cup minced ham (optional)
sprigs of fresh mint for garnish

Bring stock to a boil in a pot and drop in peas, carrots, onions, and parsnips. Reduce heat to simmer and cook until tender, about 45 minutes to 1 hour. Using a slotted spoon, remove the cooked vegetables to the bowl of a food processor and purée until smooth. Return vegetables to the sauce pan with the reserved cooking stock. Reheat soup and stir in cream and fresh mint. Garnish with optional ham and a sprig of fresh mint.
Serves 6.

ROASTED LEG OF LAMB WITH ROSEMARY

This method for cooking lamb lends itself to easy last-minute slicing and does not need as much careful watching to keep it from over-cooking—both handy features in preparing a multicourse meal.

2 tablespoons olive oil
1 whole leg of lamb, boned and
  tied, about 4 pounds
4 cloves garlic, chopped
3/4 cup chopped onions
1/2 cup sliced carrots
1/2 cup sliced celery
1 tablespoon fresh rosemary
  leaves
2 cups lamb or beef stock
salt and pepper

In a heavy-bottomed roasting pan, heat the olive oil and brown lamb on all sides. Remove the lamb to a plate and briefly sauté chopped vegetables and rosemary in the roasting pan.

Add the stock and return the lamb to the pan. Spoon some of the vegetables and sauce over the lamb, cover loosely with foil or the top of roasting pan, and bake in a preheated 375° oven for about 1 1/2 hours for medium rare. A meat thermometer should read 125–130°.

When cooking time is complete, remove lamb to a warmed serving platter and cover loosely with foil. Remove grease from pan juices, then, using a slotted spoon, remove vegetables to food processor. Purée until smooth. Pour remaining cooking juices into sauce pan, being sure to scrape up any browned bits of sauce at the bottom of the pan. Add vegetable purée to thicken sauce and reduce volume over high heat to about 2 cups of sauce. Taste for salt and pepper. Remove string from lamb and slice. Spoon a little sauce over each serving and add a sprig of fresh rosemary for garnish.

The sauce may be made up to 2 hours in advance by removing lamb 30 minutes before done and leaving lightly covered at room temperature and then following the preparation for the sauce. Be sure to add any juices that drain from the lamb as it sits in the sauce. One hour before serving time, place lamb back in a 375° oven to finish cooking for 30 to 45 minutes. Let stand 15 minutes before slicing while gently reheating the sauce in a small sauce pan.
Serves 8–10.

BALSAMIC ONIONS

2 pints fresh pearl onions
3 tablespoons unsalted butter
1/2 teaspoon sugar
3 tablespoons balsamic vinegar

Peel the onions by cutting off root ends and blanching them in boiling water for 1 minute. Drain thoroughly, then squeeze onion gently out of outer layer. Snip off any of the stem end that is dried or unsightly.

Melt the butter over moderate heat in a sauté pan and add onions and sugar. Shake the pan occasionally to keep onions from sticking and to cook evenly. After 5 minutes, add vinegar, shake pan, and cover. Reduce heat to a simmer and cook 30–40 minutes, stirring occasionally. Onions will be a rich brown and tender when done. This dish may be prepared ahead of time and gently reheated at serving time.
Serves 6–8.

SAUTÉED KALE

3 pounds kale
2 tablespoons unsalted butter
2 tablespoons olive oil
2 cloves garlic, minced
water or chicken stock as needed
salt and pepper to taste

Wash kale, drain, and remove any damaged leaves or thick stems. Coarsely chop the leaves to make handling easier. Heat a large frying pan with high sides or dutch oven and add butter and oil. When pan is hot, add the garlic. Stir briefly, then add kale. You may need to add it in batches to make room for it all. Stir for 2–3 minutes, then cover and cook at medium heat for 2–3 minutes, adding 1/4 to 1/2 cup of water or stock if too dry. Stir again and cook until kale is wilted, but still bright green. Season with salt and pepper.
Serves 6–8.

SWEET POTATO AND RICE VINEGAR SALAD

Phyllis Bostick surprised everyone with the contents of her salad bowl—the grated sweet potatoes looked just like carrot salad!

2 pounds sweet potatoes (or the equivalent of 8 cups)
1/2 cup rice wine vinegar
2 teaspoons sesame oil
1/3 cup peanut or canola oil
1 tablespoon chopped ginger, raw or pickled
4 teaspoons toasted sesame seeds
2 teaspoons sugar
1/2 teaspoon salt
cucumber or bibb lettuce for serving

Peel raw sweet potatoes and cut them into matchstick size pieces (you may use a julienne or french fry blade on a food processor). Blanch the sweet potatoes in boiling water for 1 to 2 minutes, depending on thickness. Potatoes should still be crisp in the middle. Drain and let cool.

Meanwhile, mix together the remaining ingredients and toss with the potatoes. Refrigerate the salad to blend flavors for several hours before serving. To serve, line small individual salad plates with thinly sliced cucumber or a piece of bibb lettuce. Place a spoonful of salad in the center and serve immediately.
Serves 8–10.

ANGELS ON HORSEBACK

The last course of Phyllis Bostick's family dinner is always a light savory dish. This year she chose an oyster dish, normally served as an appetizer, to end the meal.

8 ounces shucked oysters
4 ounces bacon

Select oysters that are small and bite-sized, or cut larger ones into smaller pieces. Remember, they do shrink a little while cooking. Cut bacon strips into 2-inch pieces. Wrap each oyster with a piece of bacon and secure with a toothpick. Place on a broiler pan and broil three inches from the heat, turning once after the top begins to brown. Remove when the bacon is lightly crisped. Serve immediately.
Serves 6–8.

Sweet Potato and Rice Vinegar Salad is included among the exotic luncheon dishes served on the day of the dinner.

RASPBERRY-FILLED MERINGUE HEARTS

With a bit of last-minute assembly, this very elegant dessert produces a beautiful presentation worthy of any multicourse dinner.

2 pints fresh raspberries, rinsed
and drained

MERINGUE HEARTS
4 egg whites, at room temperature
1/8 teaspoon cream of tartar
1 cup sugar

WHITE WINE SABAYON SAUCE
5 egg yolks
1/2 cup sugar
1/2 cup sweet white wine
1/4 cup framboise (raspberry
liqueur)
a dash nutmeg (optional)
3/4 cup heavy cream
1 1/2 tablespoons confectioner's
sugar

Prepare two baking sheets by cover-
ing with baking parchment paper.
Using a heart-shaped cutter or by
making a cardboard stencil, draw 16
heart-shaped outlines approximately
2 1/2 inches in width on each paper.

Place egg whites in a mixing bowl,
add cream of tartar, and mix with an
electric mixer on medium speed
until eggs hold soft peaks. Increase
beater speed to medium high and
gradually add sugar, about 1/4 cup at
a time. Continue beating until the
egg whites hold stiff peaks.

Place egg whites in a pastry bag
with medium star tube. Squeezing the
bag, outline, then fill in heart shapes
with the meringue on the parchment
papers. When each heart shape has
been completed, pipe a second layer
of meringue atop the outer edges of
eight of the heart shapes to form a
low lip for holding the raspberries and
sauce after baking.

Bake the hearts in a preheated
225° oven for 40–45 minutes, until
the meringues are firm and only
lightly colored. Leave meringues in
turned-off oven for several hours or
overnight. These meringues will
keep for several days in a tightly
sealed tin during nonhumid weather.

To make the sauce, place egg
yolks and sugar in heavy-bottomed
pot over low heat or in the top of a
double boiler over medium heat.
Whisk together until they are well
blended and pale yellow. Add wine
and liqueur and continue whisking
until sauce thickens and will heavily
coat a spoon. Take care not to let
the sauce boil (the eggs will scramble). Add optional nutmeg and chill
for several hours. When sauce is
chilled, whip cream with confectioner's sugar and fold into chilled
sauce. Keep refrigerated until ready
to assemble hearts.

ASSEMBLY
Place one bottom half of each
meringue heart on a dessert plate.
Fill with raspberries, then top with
sauce. Place the top half on the
heart and garnish with more sauce
and a few raspberries. Serve immediately.
Serves 8.

As he prepares his cooking pot, James Bentley looks like a man who has worked the land all his life.

*E*veryone is a cousin. As rich scents of hickory smoke blend with the clean smell of freshly cut grass, Bentleys and Nelsons and Trices set up tables on the front lawn, Abercrombies and Currys and Holleys lay flowers at the graves across the road, Colquitts and Grubbs carry boxes of supplies. Every so often small groups cluster to reacquaint or introduce themselves. These are the descendants of the Trice family, come together at the old homeplace in Upson County, Georgia, to celebrate the two hundredth anniversary of William Trice's birth.

Aged three months to ninety-four years, the cousins have traveled from over twenty states, from all walks of life: doctors, lawyers, farmers, truckdrivers, even an actor or two. Eight hundred descendants of William and Jane Trice are finding their way back to gather under the sheltering branches of an old oak tree, here on the very plot of ground where William and Jane carved out their homestead in 1824.

The Trice family arrived in America from England some time before William's grandfather was born in Virginia in 1740. Gradually the family began moving south. In 1823 William, then grown and married, and his wife, Jane, bought land in Upson County, built a log home just west of what is now the family cemetery, and began raising a family. Twelve of the Trices' fourteen children bore children of their own, eighty-nine grandchildren whose own grandchildren numbered in the hundreds. Generation after generation, pieces of the land, over six thousand acres at its peak, were parceled out to offspring and in economically hard times sold off; but the original homestead somehow managed to stay in family hands. Though the house itself no longer stands, the barn remains as a reminder of the traditional frame construction of an earlier day.

The reunion proper doesn't begin until tomorrow—when the handwritten genealogy charts will be mounted and the Brunswick stew ladled up from a 150-year-old family pot. But no one can wait till then to assemble. The magnetic pull of family and place is too strong. Everyone wants to help, to be part of the preparations for the formal event. Kin with license plates from Arkansas, Florida, Texas, set up their campers in nearby fields. An 84-year-old man in a bright red

Under the sheltering branches of the old oak tree, on the very plot of ground where William and Jane Trice carved out their homestead in 1824, their descendants gather to celebrate the two hundredth anniversary of William's birth.

Louise Pitts Moore, a 94-year-old descendant of Francis Ann Trice, left Upsom County when she was her granddaughter Lindsey's age. "I've never been to the Trice home site before," she says.

At first James Bentley repeats to everyone who comes near the simmering pot of Brunswick stew, "Stir the pot and your luck will change." By noon he switches his refrain: "Eat a cup of Brunswick stew and your luck will change."

shirt smiles broadly from his lawn chair, a small boy points a toy pistol at a laughing woman in a flowered blouse, two yellow-haired nine-year-olds, both answering to the name Katie, play like sisters, though they've never laid eyes on each other before.

The blessing of the pig begins at dusk, that hour before dark when the July heat begins to ease up in middle Georgia and even an over-cast Friday takes on a softened gray clarity. James Bentley announces that it is time, everyone should gather, for the official cooking is about to begin. Near the supplies table—an altar of cans of corn and tomatoes and bottles of James's homemade barbecue sauce—the cousins circle around the newly dug roasting pit. Heads bent together, they study the two pigs, intact to their glassy eyes, which lie on makeshift stretchers to roast all night above the burning hickory wood.

James raises a mint julep cup of apple brandy above the pigs' heads and offers a prayer of thanks. A compact, gray-haired man in work pants and a clean shirt (he changed behind a family car moments before), James looks like someone who has worked the land all his life. Actually, he left the farm years ago. Fresh out of college, he took a job with Georgia governor Herman Talmadge and has since been immersed in politics, including a stormy stint as the state's insurance commissioner and an unsuccessful run for the governorship. But he never completely left his parents' farm, where he still raises cattle and a few crops. For all his sophistication and business savvy, he is happiest talking about the farm and his avocation as a traditional Southern cook.

When he tosses the brandy over the pigs, a ball of fire flares up in a startling, almost sacred glow. Even weeks later James will remark in wonder at that shock of fire. The air itself seems to hold its breath in the silence. Faces beam in the ephemeral light as James laughs and kisses his wife, Gwen. The rest laugh too, a shared anticipation rippling like heat across the yard.

⤫

James and Preston Bentley and their sister, Claire Bentley Foster, instigated and organized the reunion. Direct descendants of the Trices, they grew up on this place, this land, within sight of the oak tree and cemetery. "Our father knew the background of every person buried out there," remembers James. As adults, the Bentleys continue to feel a deep sense of rootedness. "Our father's love of history was instilled in us or else we inherited it," explains Preston, a shy yet boyishly enthusiastic history buff and former teacher, as tall and slim as Jimmy is compact. Each of the Bentley children show that love of history, James with his fascination with Southern cooking, Claire with her years of genealogical research, Preston through his teaching and the eloquent correspondence he maintains with friends and relatives, particularly the elderly ones, in a telephone age. It seemed only natur-

"When we first started planning the reunion," James remembers, "I'd had a stroke and cancer and everyone said, 'James is not going to do a barbecue.' The only concession I've made is to have a gofer instead of doing it all myself."

There are few tears in the cemetery. "We were taught not to fear the cemetery," explains Preston, and there is nothing morbid or forbidding about the neat rows of graves and markers, beflagged and beflowered.

It takes four grown men to lift the pigs on their stretchers and place them on the hickory wood where they will roast all night.

Exploring Family Roots

It is easy to become cynical about old fashioned family reunions as they turn into an American institution, perhaps even a cliché. Too often organized reunions are socially awkward, emotionally hollow gatherings in motel banquet halls full of people who have dragged themselves, or been dragged, there without any real sense of familyhood. But reunions can be so much more. As independent and transient as we have become, it is reassuring to realize we are connected to others in some permanent, inviolable way. An exploration of family roots offers new appreciation for whatever history and heritage created us. And it is not that difficult to research one's family history. Check libraries and state archives for books about long-lost relatives. Many states have "family exchange files." You register the name, place of birth, and home of your last known ancestor, along with your own name and address, so other researchers scanning the file can contact you with information. Other public files that may yield information include census records, will probate and deed records, and even criminal records. Get on the mailing list of genealogical publishing houses like the Southern Historical Press in Easley, South Carolina, or the Genealogical Publishing Company of Baltimore, Maryland, to find out what books and other resources are available. Some books include listings of records available for every state and county, as well as many foreign countries. IBM- and Apple-compatible software programs exist to help in both the filing and research. Most important, talk to family members and friends. Each may offer a useful and surprising piece of the puzzle of your past.

al to share and extend their deep sense of family by bringing together the extended clan. And William Trice's two hundredth birthday was as good a time as any.

As keeper of the cemetery, where many at the reunion have relatives buried, Preston personally contacted hundreds of Trice descendants to create an ever-expanding mailing list. Claire, the manager of a bookstore in suburban Atlanta, consolidated her years of research into the family genealogy. James, the connoisseur of traditional Southern cooking, orchestrated a classic barbecue of historic proportions.

But if the Bentleys provided the initial framework, the celebration has ignited a life force of its own. "We never had any idea it would grow to such proportions," Claire exclaims in her soft, still girlish drawl.

Of those planning to attend, the Bentleys expected only a covered dish and a three-dollar donation toward expenses. Instead, as the date grew closer, contributions of money, time, and work began pouring in. Dozens of elderly cousins, many retired and on fixed pensions, sent generous checks along with lengthy, heartfelt letters of regret that poor health or the long distance would keep them away. Cousin Edward Trice offered the family a registered calf; since pork turned out to be the barbecue of choice, he sold the calf and donated the proceeds instead. A previously unknown relative, Jack Grubb, put in hours helping Preston refurbish the cemetery.

"There's been an amazing feeling of fellowship," James says, grinning. Even before the reunion proper began, "when we carried the old pot down, Father's only surviving brother drove up with some cousins in a pickup and a tractor. There's been a camaraderie, a rekindling of friendship. We cousins who grew up there a few years apart didn't get that close as kids. The Trice twins lived just down the road; we waved every day but didn't really know them. Now cousins are calling cousins. There has been a banding together of families."

With sunset Friday, more and more cousins—over two hundred by 9:30—show up and stand together sipping iced tea. Kinfolk who have not seen each other since childhood swap memories they have stored away for fifty years. At one point Ruth Trice Curry, who has remained in Upson County all her seventy-odd years, points with glee to the massive iron kettle where the Brunswick stew is to simmer tomorrow. Dating back to William Trice himself, the kettle had been an integral part of the family's working life for over a hundred years. "Why, they hid my grandfather in that pot in the Civil War," she said, repeating the story she'd heard more than half a century ago. "He was two years old. The Union soldiers came and the women were afraid so they hid him in that pot." He was William Trice's grandson.

Not only ancestors, fascinating and distant, but others are remembered this weekend. Melvin Bentley's profile, carved on his

tombstone at the right front corner of the cemetery, gazes out across his parents' land and seems to rest on the reunion itself. The youngest Bentley sibling, Melvin died over twenty years ago in an apartment fire while teaching college in Pennsylvania. He was only twenty-nine years old. James, Claire, and

The lucky Brunswick stew is ladled up from a 150-year-old family pot. "Why, they hid my grandfather in that pot in the Civil War," remembers cousin Ruth Trice Curry. "He was two years old. The Union soldiers came and the women were afraid so they hid him."

Eleanor Nelson and her daughter Melanie stay up half the night Friday preparing their covered dish, an old Upson County recipe for a carrot salad called Copper Pennies.

especially Preston, who had been very close to Melvin, repeatedly drop his name into family discussion, almost as if he were with them planning the reunion itself. Melvin, who left behind a rich legacy in his writings, has become an almost mythic spirit, symbolizing a generation of family who grew up together.

"Melvin Bentley and I were soulmates," his cousin Eleanor Nelson says with quiet emotion. They attended high school together as cheerleader and senior class president. "We learned to celebrate together. When I first got the brochure about this reunion, what hit me graphically and spiritually was how much he'd have loved this. I was so affected I had to put the brochure away in a drawer for weeks before I looked at it again."

A woman of cat-eyed vibrancy, Eleanor felt compelled, as Melvin had, to leave rural Georgia, and she now runs a business in Washington, D.C. But the pull of her roots remains strong. "Melvin used to say 'We are not ordinary,'" she explains. "Coming back here I feel I have come to the land of not ordinariness."

∽

By midmorning Saturday, cars fill the converted pony field next door. Circles of lawn chairs appear. The cemetery overflows with flowers. The picnic tables in the blue tent settle under hundreds of covered plates. And everywhere cousins greet cousins. Despite the swelling numbers, the feeling remains intimate and intense, everyone present an active participant who can literally see, touch, and taste his or her heritage.

People gather around the family charts, where the naming of their names draws cousins back again and again. No one can avoid the magic of seeing his or her name in Claire's small neat script, proud of being noted as an individual life within a framework of lives, a part of a history more thrilling as it becomes more concrete. Elderly ladies in bright summer dresses stand beside young girls in black bicycle shorts; together they study the plain white poster-board charts that trace the Trice genealogy from William and Jane up to the present. Cousin Claire took months to rule the charts by hand, then painstakingly wrote out each descendant's name. Now when cousins are not listed where they should be, Claire asks them to write themselves in.

Across the road is the stone-walled cemetery, where groups stroll and study the markers, tracing the life and death of generations. Every so often someone pauses at the headstone of an ancestor, recogniz-

ing the name from Claire's charts. Others pause at the graves of more recently buried family members, a parent or sister or child.

The land itself, still in family hands, is a solid testament to the family's endurance. Cousins from Utah or Long Island can dig their heels into the rich, red Georgia dirt, gather up a handful of rock and wildflower, look across fields William Trice himself had cleared, and know the land as their own. Standing by a clump of wild bamboo, Nancy Nelson Howard senses the physical connection. "You look around and get a real sense of where you've come from. The land is still there and it's still family land."

The naming of their names draws cousins back to the genealogy tent again and again. No one can avoid the magic of seeing his or her name in Cousin Claire's small neat script, an individual life within a framework of lives.

Across the road from the picnic area is the stone walled cemetery. "Our father knew the background of every person buried out there," recalls James with pride.

And finally, of course, there is the food, a covered dish meal beyond imagination. Hundred of bowls and platters, an incredible assortment of vegetables, salads, pickles, and casseroles, are laid out under the blue tent, not to mention 296 cakes and 35 pies.

The centerpiece is the traditional Brunswick stew, so thick you can eat it with a fork, which has been stirred for hours in the enormous Trice family kettle. Nearby the pork cooks slowly over hickory wood. The cousins pile their plates high with pork and sliced tomatoes, beans and watermelon pickles, pecan pie and iced pound cake. They walk the land, trace their names, share memories.

Jeff Holley, a young man who spent summer vacations at his grandmother's house down the road but has never felt much connection with her side of their family, stands among a group of cousins he's met for the first time.

"This has had a profound effect on what I'll pass on to my children," he says. "It's like one big living his-

A covered dish meal beyond imagination: Hundreds of bowls and platters, an incredible assortment of vegetables, salads, pickles, and casseroles brought from near and far, many cooked according to recipes handed down for generations.

tory book." He gestures toward the cemetery where his younger sister had been buried as an infant. "I imagine my mother will be buried here." Pausing, he turns toward the charts where he's just found his name. "I imagine I will be buried here too."

Jeff's grandmother, Emma Laura Prance, sits nearby in a circle of immediate family members under the shade of a big blue and white tent. Emma Laura sits erect in her wheelchair, her hands in her lap, but it is hard to tell if she is paying attention, or even listening to the conversation of her grandchildren around her. Although she raised her family just a little way down the road—her daughter Emilee has vivid memories of the Christmases and Halloweens she shared with her Bentley first cousins—Emma Laura

now lives in a nursing home confined to her wheelchair. She cries easily, her daughter says, and her strength is ebbing.

Yet even at eighty, Emma Laura Prance has an imposing presence with her white hair and strong Trice jaw. As soon as she heard the reunion was scheduled, she announced to her family that she would be making her peach conserve cake, as she has for every family gathering in memory. Never mind her ill health, the lack of kitchen facilities available to her, the physical difficulties in executing the complicated recipe. Emma Laura Prance was determined to make her cake.

So she did. Her sister Antoinette helped, taking Emma Laura from the nursing home to her own kitchen. For two days they worked together. "Sometimes I had to prop her up against the stove," Antoinette remembers, laughing and looking over to Emma Laura, who does not seem to hear.

"It was more important for Mother to make that cake than to be here herself," Emma Laura's daughter Emilee explains. "It's the last cake she'll ever bake." Standing by one of the heavily laden dessert tables, Emilee fingers the tinfoil cradling slices of her mother's cake and glances over her shoulder toward her family. "I'd love to save a piece of that cake forever."

∽

Emilee's sense of connection is shared by all who have spent even a few hours here—sitting under the tree, wandering the cemetery

across the street, walking the boundaries of the original homestead site. They are part of a family, united by history and sense of place. Celebrating their particular heritage of family and tradition, the Trice descendants evoke the universal spirit of family we all yearn to express.

By midnight Friday only a handful remain to see the pigs through the night. As they stare into the glowing embers, listening to John Reid on his dulcimer, all sense of concrete time fades. The fire, the tuneless melody from the dulcimer, the full moon—this quiet peace could have been found on the same spot of ground fifty years earlier, or one hundred and fifty.

A Covered-Dish Dinner

PRESTON BENTLEY'S CHEESE STRAWS

Almost every Southern family has its favorite recipe for cheese straws and a favorite time for serving them, too. They are as likely to be found at brunch as at tea-time or with cocktails before dinner. Preston Bentley, who likes to make them spicy, is just one of many good family cooks among the Trice descendants.

> 1 cup sifted all-purpose flour
> 1/2 teaspoon salt
> 1/4 teaspoon dry mustard
> 1/2 teaspoon cayenne pepper
>   (more if you like spicy food)
> 1/3 cup butter, melted
> 1 cup sharp cheddar cheese,
>   shredded
> 1 1/2 tablespoons ice water, or as
>   needed
> celery seed to sprinkle over top of
>   cheese straws

Preheat oven to 350°. In a medium bowl, sift flour with salt, dry mustard, and cayenne pepper. With pastry blender, cut in butter and cheese until mixture resembles coarse crumbs. Add water and stir to blend. Shape dough into ball. On lightly floured surface, roll out to 1/8 inch thick. Cut dough into strips about 3 inches long and 1/2 inch wide with pastry wheel. Sprinkle with celery seeds. Transfer strips to ungreased baking sheets and bake about 12 minutes, or until crisp. **Makes 5–7 dozen.**

FRIED CHICKEN

The Trices would have been disappointed without a sampling of some fried chicken at the reunion— and they weren't disappointed. There must have been more than a dozen offerings. This recipe relies on the directions of two master chicken fryers, Nell Adderly of Miami, Florida, and Deacon Burton of Atlanta, Georgia. An optional variation is to soak the chicken pieces in a little buttermilk before dredging in flour. It will enrich the texture and color of the crust.

> 2 whole frying chickens, cut into
>   eight pieces each (leg, thigh,
>   breast, and wing)
> 1 1/2 cups all-purpose flour
> 1 teaspoon salt
> 1/4 teaspoon pepper
> frying oil
> large cast-iron skillet

Rinse the chicken pieces thoroughly with water, then drain and pat dry. Dredge the chicken pieces in a bowl of flour mixed with salt and pepper, or shake them in a paper bag. Shake off excess flour. Pour enough cooking oil in the skillet so that it will cover at least three-fourths of the chicken when pieces are placed in skillet to cook. Heat oil to moderately hot (around 350°) and add chicken pieces, being careful not to crowd them. Fry 7–8 minutes on each side, depending on thickness, and drain on paper towels in warm oven until all the chicken pieces have been cooked. The chicken may be served hot or at room temperature. **Serves 10–12.**

SQUASH CASSEROLE

Squash is always plentiful in backyard gardens and roadside stands during the summer reunion season, and this dish is an inexpensive and satisfying one for a crowd. Elaine Ellerbee, a guest at the reunion, shared her recipe with us, and we adapted it below.

> 2 pounds yellow squash, sliced
>   1/4 inch thick
> 1 small onion, chopped
> 1 stalk celery, chopped
> 2 cups sharp cheddar cheese,
>   grated
> 1 egg, lightly beaten
> 2 cups whole milk
> 1 1/4 cups breadcrumbs (Mrs.
>   Ellerbee uses 2 cups Ritz crack-
>   er crumbs)
> 1 teaspoon salt
> 1/4 teaspoon cayenne pepper
>   (optional)
> 1 1/2 teaspoons dried sage
>   (optional)
> 3 tablespoons butter or mar-
>   garine, melted

Drop the sliced squash in a pot of boiling salted water for 5 minutes or until tender but still firm. Cool the squash under cold running water and drain thoroughly. Mix the squash together with all the

Brunswick Stew

remaining ingredients except melted butter. Place mixture in well-buttered (or use nonstick spray) casserole dish or baking pan (approximately 9 x 13 or equivalent). Drizzle butter over top and bake in a 375° oven for 30–35 minutes.

NOTE: For a lower-fat version, substitute low-fat cheddar for the regular cheddar, use skim milk in place of some or all of the milk, and reduce butter or margarine by 1 tablespoon.
Yield: 8–10 servings

SKILLET CORNBREAD

Dozens of cornbread offerings were brought to the reunion. This spicy bread makes almost a meal in itself, especially paired with a hot bowl of turnip greens or Brunswick stew.

1/4 cup all-purpose flour
1 1/3 cups coarse-ground corn-meal or harina
1/2 teaspoon baking powder
1/2 cup solid shortening
1 1/2 cups buttermilk
2 large eggs
1 medium onion, chopped

1 medium fresh jalapeño pepper with seeds and ribs removed and minced
2/3 cup canned whole-kernel corn, drained
1/3 cup sharp cheddar cheese, grated
1 tablespoon Parmesan cheese, grated (optional)

Sift together the dry ingredients into a bowl. Melt the shortening in a medium-sized iron skillet, making sure the pan is well coated and hot. In a separate bowl, beat buttermilk and eggs together and pour with the melted shortening into the dry ingredients. Mix together quickly with a wooden spoon. Add the onion, jalapeño pepper, corn, and cheddar cheese and blend together quickly. Return the mixture to the hot skillet. Sprinkle the top of the batter with the Parmesan. Bake the cornbread in a 425° oven about 30 minutes until golden brown. Cut the cornbread into wedges to serve.
Serves 8.

ABERCROMBIE BRUNSWICK STEW

Jimmy Bentley attributes the source of his popular stew recipe to the Abercrombie branch of his family. Jimmy, along with many other Southern cooks, believes the stew got its name from Brunswick County, Virginia, another ancestral home for many Georgians.

1 gallon chicken (3–4 chickens),

cooked, boned, and chopped
1/2 gallon roasted or barbecued
  pork, boned and chopped
1 quart onions, chopped
1 stick butter or pork fat
  rendered from cooked pork
1 quart chicken broth
1 gallon canned tomatoes,
  chopped
2 quarts ketchup
2 cups barbecue sauce (see
  below)
1 quart potatoes, chopped
2 gallons creamed corn
salt and black pepper

Sauté the onions briefly in the butter or fat. This can be done in a
huge iron pot over an outdoor fire or
in a heavy-bottomed pot over several burners of an indoor stove. Add
the broth and bring to a boil. Add
remaining ingredients, except for
corn and potatoes. Cook the mixture 2–3 hours to blend and thicken,
then add corn and potatoes. Be sure
to stir frequently to prevent sticking, especially at this point. Adjust
the seasonings to your taste, particularly the black pepper.
Serves 100.

ADAPTATION FOR SMALLER GROUP
1 1/2 cups chicken, cooked and
  boned
3/4–1 cup roasted or barbecued
  pork, boned and chopped
1/2 cup onions, chopped
1 tablespoon butter or pork fat
  rendered from cooked pork
1 cup chicken broth
1 1/2 cups canned tomatoes,
  chopped
1/2 cup ketchup

1/2 cup barbecue sauce
3/4 cup potatoes, chopped
2 3/4 cups creamed corn
salt and black pepper

In a heavy bottomed pot, sauté
onions briefly in the butter or fat.
Add broth and bring to a boil. Add
remaining ingredients, except for
the corn and the potatoes. Cook the
stew 1–2 hours to blend and thick-
en, then add the corn and potatoes.
Be sure to stir frequently to prevent
sticking, especially after adding
potatoes. Adjust the seasoning, particularly the black pepper.
**Makes 10 cups to serve 5 as a main
course or 10–12 as a side dish.**

BARBECUED PORK SHOULDER

*If you want to engage a Southerner
in a heated discussion, start talking
about the relative merits of regional
barbecue sauces and cooking techniques. This recipe is adapted for
common backyard grilling (you
won't have to dig a pit or sit up all
night tending coals as Jimmy
Bentley did), and it uses a vinegar-
based sauce and techniques that
are similar to those found in the
Piedmont area of North Carolina.*

4–4 1/2 pounds pork shoulder
  (Boston butt)
2 cups barbecue sauce (see p. 154)
a covered grill or smoker
charcoal
hickory wood or other favorite
  aromatic wood such as apple

Using enough charcoal to fill only
half the pan, start a fire in the pan
of a grill or smoker, leaving coals to
burn until they are at least 25 per-
cent white ash. Add the wood pieces
that have been soaked in water to
create smoke. Place the pork shoulder, which has been brought to
room temperature, fat side up on
the grill about four to six inches
from the coals. Cover the grill or
smoker and cook at a moderately
low temperature. After about 2
hours, baste the pork with barbecue
sauce and turn the meat. Add more
wood chips to increase smoke or
bolster heat if coals are cooling.
Check again and baste about every
30 to 45 minutes. Using meat temperature probe, remove when internal temperature reaches 160°. If
after 4 hours the meat is still not
done and the coals have died, you
may finish meat in a 350° oven.

Remove meat from heat and let it
stand 20–30 minutes before removing the bone and chopping the meat
coarsely. Mix the meat with enough
sauce to moisten, and serve with
extra sauce on the side.

NOTE: This method is really a cross
between traditional grilling and
smoking, as a water pan is not used.
I find that cold smoking a pork
shoulder using the water pan alone
gives it a more ham-like taste and
consistency, rather than producing
a juicy, more tender piece of meat.
But the secret remains in slow cooking at a fairly low temperature.
Larger pieces of meat, of course, will
take longer.
Serves 6–8.

JIMMY BENTLEY'S BARBECUE SAUCE

Jimmy swears by the brand labels listed here in his recipe for barbecue sauce, but you should feel free to experiment with whatever varieties are handy in your pantry. This recipe makes enough for two gallons—an appropriate amount for roasting whole pigs or giving some away to neighbors.

1 gallon White House apple cider
   vinegar
12 cups Heinz tomato sauce
1 10-ounce bottle Lea & Perrins
   Worcestershire sauce
1 1/2 cups sugar
1/4 cup salt
3–4 cups water
4 ounces McCormick's black
   pepper
1–3 teaspoons Red Rooster sauce
   or Durkee's Louisiana Hot Sauce
   or cayenne pepper to taste

Combine all ingredients in a sauce pan and simmer together 15–20 minutes. Age at least one month before using. Keeps forever.
Yield: 2 gallons

ADAPTATION FOR SMALLER GROUP
2 cups White House apple cider
   vinegar
1 1/2 cups Heinz tomato sauce
4 teaspoons Lea & Perrins
   Worcestershire sauce
6 tablespoons sugar
1/2 tablespoon salt
1/3–1/2 cup water
1 tablespoon McCormick's black

Copper Pennies

pepper
1/4–1/2 teaspoon Red Rooster
   sauce or Durkee's Louisiana Hot
   Sauce or cayenne pepper to taste

Combine all ingredients in a sauce pan and simmer together 15–20 minutes. Store finished sauce in covered jars at least one month before using. Keeps forever.
Yield: 1 quart

ELEANOR NELSON'S COPPER PENNIES

The original Trice recipe for copper pennies, from which Eleanor adapted this one, turned up at another family reunion she attended in Thomaston, Georgia, twenty years ago.

2 1/2 pounds carrots, peeled and
   sliced 1/4 inch thick
3 tablespoons tomato paste
2/3 cup sugar

2/3 cup apple cider vinegar
1/3 cup salad oil
1 teaspoon mustard, dried or
   prepared
1 teaspoon Worcestershire sauce
1 small onion, very thinly sliced
1 small green pepper, finely
   chopped

Drop the sliced carrots into a pot of boiling water and cook until tender but still firm (10 minutes). Drain well in a colander or large strainer. Beat the remaining ingredients together in a bowl, toss the sauce with carrots, and refrigerate covered until ready to serve.
Serves 8–10.

PEACH CONSERVE CAKE

You can see why Emma Laura Prance reserved this luscious cake for special occasions—it can be somewhat time consuming to produce. All claiming a "genuine family recipe," several Trice descendants pride themselves on their own version of this cake. For the following recipe, we credit Emma Laura Prance, Emilee Holley, and James Bentley.

1-2-3-4 CAKE
1 cup butter or margarine
2 cups sugar
3 cups cake flour, sifted
3 teaspoons baking powder
1/2 teaspoon salt
4 large eggs
1 cup whole milk

1 teaspoon vanilla extract
1/2 teaspoon almond extract

BURNT CARAMEL ICING
6 cups sugar
1 1/2 cups evaporated milk
1 stick of butter, softened

CONSERVE
2 cups homemade peach conserve
  or conserve made with 1
  7-ounce jar peach jam, 1/2 jar of
  orange marmalade, and 1/4 cup
  toasted chopped pecans

To make the cake, beat the butter until creamy, using an electric mixer in a large mixing bowl. Continue beating and gradually add the sugar until the batter is light and fluffy. In a separate bowl, sift the flour with the baking powder and salt and set aside. Beat one egg at a time into creamed mixture. Add flour alternately with milk (to which the flavorings have been added), beating after each addition until smooth. Pour batter into four 8-inch round greased and floured layer pans. Bake at 350° for 20–25 minutes. Cool 10 minutes on cake racks then remove from the pans to finish cooling.

For caramel icing, brown 1 cup of sugar in heavy skillet until deep brown or burnt. Set aside the caramelized sugar. In another heavy-bottomed pot, bring remaining sugar to boil with evaporated milk. Carefully add the caramelized sugar to the milk mixture. Stir vigorously, and cook to soft-boil stage. Remove icing from heat and beat in

Peach Conserve Cake

a stick of butter with electric mixer until smooth. If icing hardens before spreading on cake, soften with a teaspoon at a time of evaporated milk.

CAKE ASSEMBLY
Start by placing one layer of cake on a serving dish. Coat with caramel icing. Top with a second layer and half of the peach conserve. Top with another layer and the remaining peach conserve. Finally, add the fourth layer and cover the cake with the remaining icing.

AFTERWORD
Creating Your Own Celebrations

*W*e began our exploration of feast and celebration with great enthusiasm but also a little trepidation. Frankly, we worried—given all the talk these days about rootlessness, materialism, the general shallowness of contemporary life, we feared the celebrations we'd heard so much about would not live up to our expectations, would offer only joyless extravaganza or rituals rigid and rote. To our great delight, our fears were unfounded. The capacity to celebrate remains strong and infinitely renewable. At the feast tables we joined, traditions and rituals resonated with symbolic meaning, and participants clearly relished the festive spirit.

We discovered that while methods and styles of celebration are remarkably varied, patterns do form and are good guidelines as we try to create and invigorate our own celebrations.

It helps if one strong personality acts as a unifying force, at least when a tradition is first getting off the ground. By initiating and orchestrating her dinners, Phyllis Bostick brought her children back to being a family. Gil Watson moved a house piece by piece to give his cousins a sense of homeplace. Gladys Widdis played a crucial role in establishing Cranberry Day as an official tribal holiday, although she has since passed much of the responsibility for its celebration on to younger Wampanoags.

That sharing of responsibility is ultimately what brings a community or family together. The Bentleys were amazed at the outpouring of support from distant relatives, and their inclusion in the preparations created a sense of familyhood that made their reunion that much more meaningful. Glenda Lubrano's altar was particularly moving because it displayed the efforts of a community of women who baked and talked and laughed together for weeks. In fact, at all the gatherings we attended, everyone's active participation gave the event its sense of larger purpose by creating a bond of mutual commitment.

Such participation can also make celebration less exhausting. We hope we've shown that while a certain amount of energy and time is necessary, creating a celebratory feast need not be a backbreaking endeavor. Spreading around responsibility, especially for food preparation, limits the effort each individual must commit and makes the experience more fun as a shared event. Iris Gomez was relaxed and happy—not at all stressed—by Gabriela's baby welcoming barely two weeks after her birth because friends pitched in and did the physical work. Shortcuts are allowed, and sometimes advised. Few of the meals we describe are more elaborate than the Thanksgiving dinner in Cleveland, but Iris Bailin showed no shame at using paper napkins.

Given the realities of life today, flexibility is essential for celebrations, and celebrants, to survive. When Phyllis Bostick's plans for a Sunday picnic were rained out, Phyllis and her kids created a cheerful picnic indoors.

And while ritual must be taken seriously for a tradition to endure, spontaneity plays a large part in creating the joy that brings tradition to life. At the Madorskys' Passover Seder, the service was followed closely, but interrupted repeatedly by questions and good-natured banter. At the Nanjis' Kwanza celebration, the unexpected arrival of Taji Nanji's brother just as the gathering was about to discuss the importance of family enriched the ceremony immeasurably. Each celebration had a moment, unexpected and more fitting than anything that could be planned, that energized everyone involved.

∽

In preparing a multicourse dinner, remember that the object is not for you, the host or hostess, to be too exhausted or preoccupied to celebrate. Consider the following suggestions:

Enlist help. Ask a different guest to help with each course. This help can include preparing a specific dish or sauce, doing some last-minute stirring, or clearing the table and washing the dishes between their assigned courses. Ask other guests to bring a beverage for one course.

Plan a menu with many items that can be prepared well in advance or that require only last-minute preparation. Alternating hot and cold dishes helps, especially when juggling oven and stove-top space. And keep portions small—not only will you prevent stuffing your guests, but your refrigerator will be less crowded, too. Choose recipes carefully. Homemade stocks for sauces, soups, and stews can be prepared at least a month in advance. Many dessert ingredients can be made and frozen a week or so in advance without loss of flavor.

Consider purchasing one or two well-prepared or unusual ready-made items from a local bakery or deli. A birthday cake, freshly baked breads or cookies, or an appetizer such as pâté or a seafood sausage can go a long way toward rounding out an elaborate menu without adding labor or detracting from your guests' enjoyment.

Select all china, glassware, and serving pieces in advance and label them. Set the table two to three days in advance if possible. Write out a chronological task list of the evening's preparations schedule and order of service. Underline or highlight important tasks. It's easy to lose your concentration while visiting with your guests—so why worry about it. Your list can help keep you on track without missing the fun.

Finally, *start dinner early* so there's plenty of time to savor each course and adequate time to prepare the next one.

∽

The act of celebration is universal, and it comes in so many forms. For every gathering we included, we can point to another we wanted to chronicle as well.

■ The Midsummer's Eve on Sonny and Dale Nimrod's Iowa farm — more than one hundred family members and neighbors decorate a 35-foot maypole with real wildflowers and share a Scandinavian potluck feast.

■ Ching Ming — Chinese families visit their ancestors' graves to honor them. While picnicking on poached chicken, suckling pig, and other favorite traditional foods, each family burns paper replicas of its ancestor's interests when alive in order to send them to the ancestor.

■ The Arrango household in New Mexico — as Polly Arrango says, "Everyone knows to come on Sunday night" for the weekly family supper of chicken and fixings.

No one type of community, no one ethnic group or religion, has an edge when it comes to celebration. Money, education, social standing are equally irrelevant. What counts is setting time apart from the daily routine and sharing the feast with family and friends.

BIBLIOGRAPHY

Agel, Jerome, and Jason Shulman, *The Thanksgiving Book*. New York: Dell, 1987.

Applebaum, Diana Karter. *Thanksgiving*. New York: Facts on File, 1984.

Beard, James. *James Beard's American Cookery*. Boston: Little, Brown, 1972.

Brody, Jane. *Jane Brody's Good Food Book*. New York: Bantam, 1987.

Burnett, Bernice. *Holidays*. New York: Franklin Watts, 1983.

Cardozzo, Arlene Rossen. *Jewish Family Celebrations*. New York: St. Martin's, 1974.

Carey, Diana, and Judy Large. *Festivals Family and Food*. Gloucestershire: Hawthorn Press, 1982.

Chambers, Wicke, and Spring Asher. *The Celebration Book*. New York: Harper and Row, 1979.

Child, Julia. *The Way to Cook*. New York: Knopf, 1989.

Clayton, Bernard, Jr. *The Complete Book of Breads*. New York: Simon & Schuster, 1990.

Cox, Harvey. *The Feast of Fools*. Cambridge, Mass.: Harvard University Press, 1969.

Fisher, Aileen. *Easter*. New York: Thomas Y. Crowell, 1986.

Frazier, James G. *The Golden Bough*. New York: Avenel Books, 1890.

Geffen, Alice M., and Carole Berglie. *Food Festival*. New York: Pantheon, 1986.

Goodman, Philip. *The Passover Anthology*. Philadelphia: The Jewish Publication Society of America, 1961.

Gourmet Cooking from Syria and Lebanon. St. George's Church Guild.

Gourmet's Best Desserts. Conde Nast Books. New York: Random House, 1987.

Hazan, Marcella. *The Classic Italian Cookbook*. New York: Harper & Row, 1973.

Herbst, Sharon Tyler. *Food Lover's Companion*. Hauppauge, N.Y.: Barron's Educational Series, 1990.

Hole, Christina. *Christmas and Its Customs*. New York: M. Barrow, 1958.

———. *Easter and Its Customs*. New York: M. Barrow, 1961.

Humphrey, Theodore C., and Lin T. Humphrey. *We Gather Together*. Ann Arbor, Mich.: UMI Research Press, 1988.

King, Louise Tate, and Jean Stewart Wexler. *The Martha's Vineyard Cookbook*. Chester, Conn.: Globe Pequot Press, 1989.

Konner, Melvin, Marjorie Shostak, and Boyd Eaton. *The Paleolithic Prescription*.

Linton, Ralph and Adelin. *The Lore of Birthdays*. New York: Henry Schuman, 1952.

McDougal, John A. *The McDougal Program*. New York: Penguin Books, 1990.

Nathan, Joan. *The Children's Jewish Holiday Kitchen*. New York: Schocken Books, 1987.

Peck, M. Scott. *The Road Less Traveled*. New York: Simon & Schuster, 1978.

Penner, Lucille Recht. *The Thanksgiving Book*. New York: Hastings House, 1986.

Perl, Lila. *Candles, Cakes, and Donkey Tails*. New York: Ticknor and Fields, 1984.

Pieper, Josef. *In Tune with the World: A Theory of Festivity*. New York: Harcourt, Brace, and World, 1963, 1965 (trans.).

Pinderhughes, John. *Family of the Spirit Cookbook*. New York: Simon & Schuster. 1990.

Union Haggadah, The. The Central Conference of American Rabbis, 1923.

INDEX